# Reengineering through Cycle Time Management

## Wayne L. Douchkoff
*Executive Vice President, Professionals for Technology*

## Thomas E. Petroski
*Director, Professionals for Technology*

**PT Publications, Inc.**
3109 45th Street, Suite 100
West Palm Beach, FL 33407-1915

Library of Congress Cataloging in Publication Data

Douchkoff, Wayne L.
    Reengineering through cycle time management /Wayne L.
Douchkoff, Thomas E. Petroski.
                        p.  cm.
    Includes bibliographical references and index.
    ISBN 0-945456-12-3 (hardcover)
    1. Product life cycle. 2. Product management. 3. Time
management.  I. Petroski, Thomas E. 1948-    . II. Title.
HF5415.155.D68    1996
658.5'6—dc20                                        95-26503
                                                        CIP

# Table of Contents

Preface                                                          Page *vii*

Chapter 1:  How to Get Started                                   Page   1

Chapter 2:  Reducing the Design
            and Development Cycle                                Page  31

Chapter 3:  Manufacturing Technology                             Page  53

Chapter 4:  Supply Base Management                               Page  81

Chapter 5:  Marketing/Sales/Customer
            Service Cycle                                        Page  93

Chapter 6:  Lessons Learned                                      Page 113

Chapter 7:  Combating Resistance                                 Page 127

Chapter 8:  Administration
            Cycle Time Management                                Page 137

Chapter 9:  Finance Cycle Time                                   Page 147

Chapter 10: Computers in Cycle Time
            Management                                           Page 161

Index                                                            Page 171

# PREFACE

We decided to write this book when we realized that Pro-Tech had been practicing and preaching, not theorizing and discussing, Cycle Time Management for a number of years. While others were talking about Just-In-Time, Supplier Certification or Total Quality Management as cure-all programs, we were emphasizing the need to make these very important tools and philosophies part of a larger effort. That larger effort focused on eliminating as many wasteful activities as possible and seeking continuous improvement throughout the cycle time of any set of activities. And what is more, we have never treated a set of activities which was under study as an island unto itself in the organization. We have always stated that a company is more like a continent crisscrossed by highways which form an internal network of suppliers and customers.

The network, of course, extends to the external world of suppliers and customers as well. In fact, we have always believed that suppliers should be full partners in the efforts to orient a company to the continuous improvement ethic. That belief has been the foundation of our highly successful Supply Management process which we have helped to implement throughout North America and Europe. Even though we have sold many copies of our book, *Supplier Certification II: A Handbook for Achieving Excellence Through Continuous Improvement* (PT Publications, West Palm Beach, FL), we were not content to rest upon our laurels. We added *Supply Management Toolbox* (PT Publications, West Palm Beach, FL) and *Power Purchasing* (PT Publications, West Palm Beach, FL), a comprehensive book about Supply Management with Carl Cooper, Senior Applications Consultant, at Motorola University. Why do we keep adding and polishing? Because how could we teach about continuous improvement and customer satisfaction if we ourselves didn't strive to publish books that the business community needs?

We like to think, however, that we have been on the right track from the beginning. In our first book, *Made in America: The Total Business Concept*, (PT Publications, West Palm Beach, FL), we identified Just-In-Time and Total Quality Control (JIT/TQC) as a "quest for the causes of wasted time, money and labor and an attempt to destroy what we refer to as the "Ubiquitous RE-" — rework, repair, reject, refuse and so on." Later, we go on to define JIT/TQC as a mindset and a total business philosophy, but we did not stop there in our evolution of this key area in Cycle Time Management .

Before long, we began to see that Total Quality Management (TQM), although a worthwhile goal, was somewhat limited in today's marketplace. TQM, as many apply it, focuses on just the manufacturing and quality assurance areas of an organization. For it to be truly "total" in the newly emerging environment of agile organizations, TQM needed to embrace all functions and drive out all nonvalue-added activities. This is precisely the point at which *Reengineering through Cycle Time Management* enters the picture.

It is also the point where our activities in educating and training companies about Activity Based Costing (ABC) comes into play. In our recently published book, *Activity Based Costing: The Key to World Class Performance* (PT Publications, West Palm Beach, FL), we identify ABC as a natural partner for all of the latest business philosophies. Its emphasis on identifying cost drivers and allocating them to the proper products and services is essential to driving out nonvalue-added activities. ABC provides organizations with a costing system that generates the information you need to run your company in the most efficient and profitable manner possible.

So far, we have talked about a great deal of change, a sometimes difficult evolution from traditional practices to more innovative ones. At Pro-Tech, we have always believed that you can be lean by yourself, but that it takes partners to be agile. As we have pointed out in our book, *People Empowerment: Achieving Success from Involvement* (PT Publications, West Palm Beach, FL), your most valuable partners are the people who work in your company. This is not an empty slogan. Organizations need to involve and empower their workers, both blue-collar and white-collar, in order to unleash the latent skills and talent locked up in their minds and experiences. Using teams to brainstorm and problem solve is a key part of Cycle Time Management.

We have mentioned agile manufacturing several times in this

preface. It is a recent concept, but one that we think is vital to your survival in the marketplace of the 21st century. And we believe that Cycle Time Management is the operative philosophy which will allow us to create organizations that respond to precisely what the customer wants. Agile manufacturing requires the inclusive and synchronous style that forms the core of Cycle Time Management. This new business style will place an emphasis on zero inventory, zero waste, fast response times and short production cycles. Only a company that works together can achieve World Class levels.

At Pro-Tech, we believe that we have helped clients evolve for three reasons:

1) We teach the need to be proactive, not reactive. That's another way of saying "continuous improvement."
2) We advocate education and training at all levels of an organization. Everybody must contribute and everybody has something to contribute.
3) We stress management commitment and ownership. Cycle Time Management is nothing less than a new vision and strategic direction for an organization.

This book is written with those same ideas in mind. We show you the tools and other techniques at your disposal which you can use to reduce cycle time and improve performance. As always, we strive to combine theory and application because we feel that it is the most effective way to impart knowledge.

The American economy is based on manufacturing and its related support industries, but this base is being eroded by global competition which is becoming more and more keen with each passing month. If we are to stay competitive, we must change immediately. The plan we have presented in this book shows you the best path to the future. Nothing which we have described is outside your ability to do. We know this is true because the small, medium and large clients of Pro-Tech have all successfully implemented various parts of our Continuous Improvement Process. It is not easy. It requires an investment in time, money and resources. But, the return on those investments could be more than your long-term competitiveness. It could be the continued survival of your enterprise.

*Peter L. Grieco, Jr.*
*West Palm Beach, FL*

# ACKNOWLEDGMENTS

We would like to thank all of our clients for their good ideas, common sense and courage which were used to strive for continuous improvement. This book is their story of meeting one of America's most serious challenges. Special thanks go out to all of our colleagues at Pro-Tech who have challenged us and contributed their stories to this book. We thank them all for the time they took to review each chapter and make suggestions.

A special mention is reserved for the capable and hard-working office staff who are always there for us as we travel across the country and to foreign countries. Much appreciation is due to Steven Marks for his creative editorial assistance. We wish also to thank Kevin Grieco for his design of our book cover.

We at Pro-Tech would also like to acknowledge in advance all the people who use this book and its ideas to bring their organizations into the 21st century. These people command our respect for their tireless efforts to bring costs under control and to make their companies and facilities into World Class institutions.

# Chapter One:
# How to Get Started

Let us begin this book with a hypothetical situation, but one with which you can relate and identify to some degree. We represent a resource company which assists other companies in the improvement of their operating performance at all levels, both in administrative and manufacturing areas. We have found that it is rare for a person to come straight to the point in addressing cycle time opportunities or the change process required to institutionalize cycle time. Unfortunately, our culture seems to have conditioned people to be afraid to ask for help because they fear being seen as stupid or weak. We remind people who contact us that anyone can fail by themselves, but that it takes partners to be successful. Partners, we add, with a strategic plan.

But the call we got early one Monday morning was different. This caller got right to the point and was not embarrassed to paint a realistic picture of her company's situation.

"I'm Mary Andrews," she said, "and I'm the president of a seven-year-old hi-tech firm with $87 million in sales. We manufacture electronic telecommunications products that we call Blackboxes. We build them in a number of configurations, styles and options as well as provide service and training to our customers. In addition, we have an in-house technical service group which helps customers identify and explore new applications for our products."

"Who are your customers?" we asked her. Customer satisfaction is the bedrock of all business activities, so we like to know right away who our clients sell to.

1

# Reengineering through Cycle Time Management

"We are pretty evenly divided between consumers, the military and industry," Ms. Andrews quickly replied. "It has been a conscious strategic decision on our part not to put all our eggs in one basket. The problem isn't with these ratios, but with the fact that are experiencing a small, but steady decrease in the number of new customers we are landing. That has me worried about the future."

I remember thinking that this would be an excellent person to work with. She was forward-looking. It would not be difficult to convince her of the merits of cycle time reduction and agile manufacturing. Whether she knew it or not, her company was poised to take that next step, both in the administrative and manufacturing areas.

"I'm afraid," she continued, "that somebody who is flexible and has a quicker-to-market time will come along and start eroding our customer base. I want our company to be as quick on its feet as the little guys. We can't afford to lose one single customer or to get into a costly price war."

I explained to her that it has always been our philosophy to eliminate or reduce wasteful activities and seek continuous improvement throughout the cycle time of any set of activities. Just-In-Time, Supply Management and Total Quality Management are all very useful tools, but all too often companies treat them as isolated programs. We have taught that it is never wise to treat any part of your business as an island. A company is more like a continent crisscrossed by highways which form a network between internal suppliers and customers as well as links to external suppliers and customers.

"You anticipated my question," Ms. Andrews said with a laugh. "I've been reading a number of articles lately, including yours, about Cycle Time Reduction and I liked what you had to say. We may be doing well now, even quite well, but I treat the problems I've described as very serious. I want my company to survive and prosper. That won't happen by standing still, so how do I get started?"

We now had the privilege of working with a new client, the Blackbox Company. In some of the coming chapters, we will revisit this company in order to make points about the topic under discussion. But let's now turn our attention to an overview of Cycle Time Management (CTM) and how it can be implemented throughout an organization. Then, we will look at the process you need to undergo in order to institutionalize CTM.

# What is Cycle Time Management?

If the definition of cycle time is the time that elapses from the signaling of a customer need to customer satisfaction, then Cycle Time Management is nothing less than the integration of all the activities in an organization under one operating philosophy. What is that operating philosophy? It is that a company must adopt business practices which allow it to build better products faster than its competitors. Furthermore, all of these business practices should serve to shorten cycle time. In so doing, we can then reduce or eliminate waste, improve quality, asset utilization and customer service, and shorten the time it takes to bring a product or service to market.

That's a big promise, but entirely possible when a company makes Cycle Time Management a way of life in the organization. Although institutionalization is possible at any type of company, it is never easy. We expect the process to normally take two to three years in order to reach an optimal level. Once that is accomplished, we then set the goal of continuously improving upon that level. Standing still in the business world is the same as falling behind, and sometimes out of existence, as the competition passes us by.

In our own organization, Cycle Time Management grew out of our activities in a number of areas with clients and companies wanting to be faster and more flexible. Like us, all came to see that the critical element in Just-In-Time (JIT), Total Quality Management (TQM), Supply Management, Set-up Reduction and so on was time. In JIT, for example, lowering inventory levels had the effect of exposing hidden problems. Cycle Time Management identifies barriers to shorter cycle times and, in doing so, exposes the wasteful activities that steal valuable time from a company's ability to reach customer satisfaction. Similarly, these techniques or tools showed how large lot sizes and long set-up times contributed to longer cycle times and less than ideal quality levels. When we reviewed lead times, we found that the only time when work is actually done is during run or process time. Move, wait, queue and set-up time were all nonvalue-added activities.

Long ago, we realized why the focus had to be on cycle time. Cycle Time Management allows companies to create organizations that respond precisely to what a customer wants via shorter design, development, production, sales, marketing, and operations cycles. Cycle time, as you can see, is not one monolithic wheel that keeps turning and turning. It is made up of smaller cycles like those just identified. And each of these cycles breaks down into even smaller cycles of activities. In the future, only the companies which are able to map all the processes, large or small, in their organization will prosper. The marketplace will demand customized products in less and less time. At Motorola University, where we teach, Cycle Time Management has been made mandatory for all the company's functions. Measurements, goals and objectives are spelled out on a card carried by most of the staff. Cycle Time Management is not an elective, it is a core requirement.

Cycle Time Management goes through a six-step cycle of its own. This cycle is basically the same for every department, function or activity in your company. The steps are:

1) Determine a starting point. You can do this in several ways, but the following three are most prevalent:

   a) Calculate the theoretical cycle time by mapping the process and adding up the time for each activity or process as if there were no time taken for set-ups, stoppages or waiting. Use this figure as an ideal level to be approached. That level is, of course, impossible to reach. But many experts suggest trying to reach an optimal level which is some multiple of the theoretical time. For manufacturing, they recommend that optimal cycle time be two or three times theoretical. For white-collar and service companies, the multiplier is five to ten.

   b) Determine and establish your current baseline. How long is each activity in your cycle time now? Use this figure as a base level from which you can improve and set new goals.

   c) Benchmark the cycle time from the best of the best, World Class companies in each business area. Find a company which performs the same or a similar activity and use this figure as a goal to attain. Each activity may be represented by a different benchmarked company which may not even be in your industry. The choice is determined by whoever is the best in that activity area. The classic example is of Xerox benchmarking the warehousing and shipping activities of L.L. Bean. We will be discussing benchmarking in more detail later in the chapter.

2) Gather information about each cycle. What cycles feed into it? What downstream cycles does it feed? Utilize process flow mapping. The point is to understand each element of the cycle as fully as possible, and this can only be accomplished when the information you need is complete.

3) Begin examining and analyzing the various elements and activities in the cycle. Pay particular attention to the areas in between these elements. These "white areas" between one step in a process and another step are often the places where the most improvements can be made. They are so often overlooked that bad habits and practices have been able to accumulate to the detriment of the total cycle time. This is where you will find most of your bottlenecks and disconnects. Don't ignore the identifiable processes, however. The goal of this step is to analyze all of the cycle's components and then to begin brainstorming solutions.

4) Begin problem solving. We highly recommend teams for this activity. If you wish to see our suggestions for the dynamics of team problem solving, read Wayne Douchkoff's book, *People Empowerment: Achieving Success from Involvement* (PT Publications, Inc., West Palm Beach, FL). If you want to look over how to use a team to problem-solve on more technical matters, then read *Set-Up Reduction: Saving Dollars with Common Sense* (PT Publications, Inc., West Palm Beach, FL).

5) Develop a strategy and a plan and put both into action. Reduce or eliminate redundant or ineffective steps using the tools to be discussed throughout this book.

## Reengineering through Cycle Time Management

6) Most important is to measure each cycle time area in order to determine your progress. We must provide feedback so people in our company can steer a course to even higher levels of achievement. Feedback and measurements are critical. In our opinion, they are the backbone of any attempt to institutionalize Cycle Time Management at your company.

# Continuous Improvement Process
# — A Key Feedback Cycle

One of the principal benefits of Cycle Time Management is the opportunity to generate more of the feedback mentioned in the sixth step above than can be generated in conventional situations. It stands to reason that the more times you can run through a cycle in a given period of time, the more opportunities you have to learn from the improvements you make during each iteration. We call our feedback cycle the Continuous Improvement Process (CIP), and it is diagrammed in Figure 1-1.

The left side of the chart shows the Development/Preparation phase. It consists of four steps:

**Cycle Time Education — communicate a consistent message about Cycle Time Management throughout the company.**

**Strategic Plan — establish goals, objectives and mission; identify where opportunities exist and what benefits will ensue from engaging in the cycle time process.**

**Identify Customer Requirements — use customer surveys to communicate and define customer needs and expectations.**

**Action Plan — develop a one-year plan (not a five-year plan) which shows the directions, objectives and goals for success.**

The right side of the chart shows the Implementation Process which consists of six steps. In Step one, you form teams in both the manufacturing and administrative areas which are required to address cycle time issues. The next step is for each team to map the

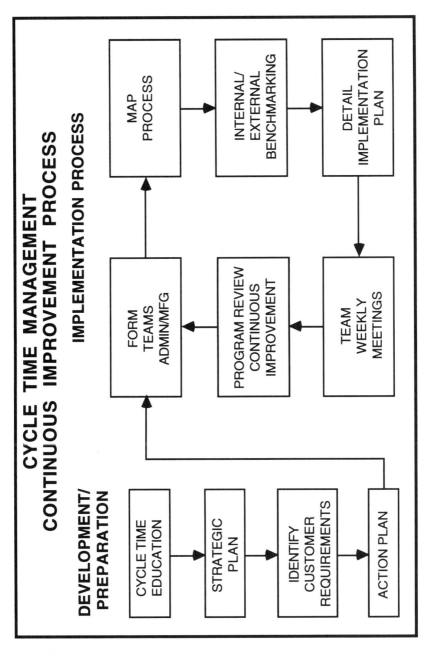

Figure 1-1.

## Reengineering through Cycle Time Management

process in order to understand the task. Next, we need to benchmark both internal business areas and external World Class companies to establish goals and create standards of performance. In the fourth step, the individual teams decide on a course of action which will meet the parameters set by a steering committee. The fifth step is to schedule weekly team meetings where problems are discussed and potential solutions are weighed. In the last step, the team takes the results of its efforts and uses them to direct and support the next effort.

The point of these six steps is to keep the process ongoing, so that there is continuous improvement, and to focus the whole process at the lowest organizational level. We must remind ourselves that these are the people who know how to identify and reduce cycle time. The key to cycle time reduction is teamwork. You know you are on the right track when people start looking at ways to improve cycle times as part of their normal, day-to-day business activities.

# What to Expect from Cycle Time Management

Because Cycle Time Management is driven by a process of continuous improvement whereby teams brainstorm solutions, you can expect to spend a small amount of money and use equally small amounts of company resources. We believe that all teams should receive training in cost/benefit analysis so that they can find low cost or no cost solutions. Automation and new software systems, for example, are often high cost solutions, and we have found that either they are not necessary or they aggravate the situation by automating wasteful activities.

What you can expect from Cycle Time Management is a factor of what your company asks of itself. Consider what demands Motorola is making upon itself in the following mission statement:

### MANAGING FOR WORLD CLASS QUALITY

"Motorola is engaged in a very competitive marketplace. We will not grow if we continue to focus only on what we have done well in the past.

"We will achieve Six Sigma and beyond results in

**everything we do, and strive for a 10-times reduction in
defects every two years.**

**"We will apply cycle time reduction techniques to all
elements of our business, with a goal of 10-times
improvement in cycle time in the next five years."**

MOTOROLA

In effect, Motorola is saying that cycle time is reduced effectively only if no element of their business is viewed as isolated from
other elements in the company. The philosophy of Cycle Time
Management is about bringing cohesiveness, unity and integration
into a company. That requires, first, that companies embrace a Six
Sigma philosophy: defects will not be tolerated at any point in the
process. Second, companies must comply with smaller lot sizes and
on-time delivery. The objective is to utilize material as soon as it
arrives at the receiving dock (Ship-To-Stock) and eventually to have
material shipped directly to the line (Ship-To-WIP). Excess material
handling equipment, personnel and time spent on the movement of
material is what we need to avoid. These are nonvalue-added
activities.

The intent of cycle time reduction is to get the right activity to
the right place at the right time so that every procedure or operation
adds value to the product. An important area to tackle when reducing cycle time is lead time, as we mentioned earlier. The majority of
lead time is taken up by queues. You can greatly reduce queue time
by reviewing all of the mapped processes and eliminating those
steps in which there is no real work, steps which simply eat up
time. Along with queue reduction, you should also address set-
up reduction. The two comprise the major areas of opportunity.
Shorter lead times result in a higher inventory turnover rate and a
greater return on assets. Our goal is to attack as quickly as possible
all elements of lead time and related tasks and functions that are not
real work (value added). We do this throughout the organization.

You can expect that whatever results you obtain from Cycle
Time Management will stay with you. When a Cycle Time Management process is used in conjunction with the Continuous Improvement Process, they combine to change the company culture. We will
be discussing culture in much more detail in Chapter Seven. For now,
let's look at some of the quantitative results of various cycle time

## Reengineering through Cycle Time Management

reduction activities. In manufacturing cycle time, for example, we have helped companies achieve the following:

### MANUFACTURING CYCLE TIME ACHIEVEMENTS

| ACTIVITY | IMPROVEMENT | INDUSTRY |
|---|---|---|
| Punch Press | 45 minutes to 45 seconds | Drapery hardware |
| Screw insertion | 36 minutes to 9 seconds | Aerospace |
| Processing line | 4 hours to 7 minutes | Food processing |
| CNC milling machine | 73 minutes to 1 minute | Aerospace |
| Cosmetics line | 8 hours to 10 minutes | Cosmetic |
| CNC chucker | 118 minutes to 12 minutes | Machine shop |
| Circuit board line | 6 hours to 13 minutes | Computer |
| Forming press | 150 minutes to 6 minutes | Automotive |
| Lathe | 65 minutes to 8 minutes | Motor |
| Welder | 3 hours to 8 minutes | Power transformers |
| Line changeover | 4 hours to 0 hours | Medical devices |

The above results are for one area of a company's operations. Think of what can be accomplished when this is a company- or function-wide effort. The figures below show what some companies have accomplished when they applied Cycle Time Management techniques to the new product development cycle.

### U.S. FIRMS' PROGRESS IN REDUCING NEW PRODUCT DEVELOPMENT CYCLE

| FIRM | PRODUCT | RESULTS |
|---|---|---|
| Honeywell | Thermostat | 4 yrs. to 1 yr. |
| Navistar | Trucks | 5 yrs. to 2.5 yrs. |
| IBM | Printers | 4 yrs. to 2 yrs. |
| Hewlett-Packard | Printers | 4.5 yrs. to 22 mos. |
| Northern Telecom | Digital switches | 20-50% reduction |
| Motorola | Pagers | 3 yrs. to 18 mos. |
| Brunswick | Outboard motors | 25-30% reduction |
| Xerox | Copiers | 4-5 yrs. to 2 yrs. |
| 3M | Microfilm readers | 3 yrs. to 2.5 yrs. |
| Hat Brands | Stetson hats | 70% reduction |

No discussion of Cycle Time Management and the integration of all company activities would be complete without defining Cycle

Time Management's relationship to the future. In many ways, Cycle Time Management is the method by which a company can become World Class. Although the discussion that follows is primarily about manufacturing, you will readily see that its principles apply to all kinds of companies. In fact, one of the tenets of agile manufacturing is to run your company more like a service organization.

# Agile Manufacturing and Cycle Time Management

Agile manufacturing is a concept which has only recently arrived on the scene, but we think it will be vital to your survival in the marketplace of the 21st century. And we believe that Cycle Time Management is the operative philosophy which will allow you to create organizations that respond precisely to what a customer wants. Agile manufacturing requires the inclusive and synchronous style that forms the core of Cycle Time Management. Like the philosophies of cycle time reduction, this new business style will place an emphasis on zero inventory, zero waste, fast response times and short production cycles.

Many of you may have already heard of agile manufacturing from stories about Japan's quest for the three-day car. The production of a car in three days is an example of their version of agile manufacturing as developed by that country's Japanese Manufacturing 21 Project. There are examples closer to home as exemplified by General Motor's Saturn, Benetton and Wal-Mart. Some of the agile ideas they are pursuing are described below:

<u>AGILE IDEAS</u>

**SATURN**
**In planning production, Saturn "images" or creates stock orders for its dealers. The retailer then has the opportunity to change the order in real-time according to the desires of its customers. The new specifications are directly reported to production scheduling at the Saturn plant.**

**BENETTON**
**Instead of dying yarn and then knitting the sweaters, Benetton**

produces finished sweaters in neutral colors and then dyes them to meet the market demand for colors.

## WAL-MART
Wal-Mart lets individual stores order directly from suppliers. Using this method, Wal-Mart maintains high service standards with 25 percent of the inventory. The company has also been able to cut restocking time from 6 weeks to 36 hours.

In order to become agile like the companies above, all administrative and operational activities must be analyzed to ensure that they flow seamlessly from upstream suppliers to downstream customers in the shortest possible time. Cycle Time Management is thus a key tool in achieving significant results in that regard. The agile organization will need to develop the following capabilities of Cycle Time Management:

### Capability 1

Companies intent on implementing agile methodologies will need an accounting and finance system which assigns costs more accurately to products and services and which provides management with the cost information needed to make strategic decisions. Activity Based Costing will be the system to meet these needs.

### Capability 2

Movement will also need to be made toward lowering costs by integrating information systems and designing equipment so that set-up time simply involves reprogramming the machine. There should be no physical removal of tools or dies, for example. The machine would reconfigure itself to the new job according to the instructions it receives from the company's integrated data base. This cost-cutting would also be reflected in the design of modular production facilities and products. Some futurists see the possibility of buying one car in your lifetime. As parts wear out or get improved, they would be replaced at "service centers." Even style changes would be done by outfitting your vehicle with new body panels.

### Capability 3

Quality must be designed into the product and the process at the same time, thus guaranteeing that the product is producible and conforms to customer requirements.

**Capability 4**

We have always tried to make it the philosophy of Pro-Tech that you can become a lean organization by yourself, but that it takes partners to become agile. Agility requires key alliances with supplier/partners to ensure a continuous flow of quality materials, in the required quantities, at the right time. To achieve this level of support, World Class organizations must implement Supply Management techniques such as Supplier Certification.

**Capability 5**

Information and time in the agile organization must be managed in much the same way that JIT methodologies have managed inventories. Cycle Time Management needs to be employed in order to reduce the number of ways information is channeled through an organization by reducing the number of layers of management involvement. In other words, decisions should be forced down to the lowest possible level in the organization.

Agile manufacturing and Cycle Time Management are, as you can see, almost synonymous. One of our clients once remarked that all you need to do to manage cycle time is implement Set-Up Reduction, Total Quality Management, Supply Management, Activity Based Costing, People Involvement and Empowerment, and Concurrent Engineering. That's a good start, we told him, but you won't get anywhere unless you know how to enact these processes at your company. What does a company need to make Cycle Time Management work?

# How to Make Cycle Time Management Work in Your Company

The best way to make Cycle Time Management work in your company is not to implement it as a program, but to institutionalize it. By institutionalizing, we mean making Cycle Time Management part of your company's culture, not a program which everybody signs on to and then forgets after a few months. Culture change requires the reengineering of a company, perhaps even the formation of a permanent state of reengineering. That's the attitude taken by Peter Jacobi, the president of Levi Strauss International, the world's largest apparel-maker. Even though the company is expanding markets and lines and racking up record sales years, Jacobi is worried about the company's level of service to retailers. To address this issue, the company has put a $400 million effort into motion to restock retailers in three days and to get new clothing into stores within one month, instead of the current six months. That's not a program; that's a way of doing business, and that's the type of culture change which will be needed to survive in the coming agile marketplace.

A new organizational culture is required in order to facilitate the changes necessary for the future. The culture must be one in which people feel free to take the initiative in approaching upper management with problems and ideas for solving them. An "open-ear" policy is an integral part of this new environment. We say "open-ear" because an "open-door" policy often doesn't have the desired result of producing a culture of listening. In fact, the eventual outcome of this new culture of which we speak is to have teams which are self-governing. Such teams don't need to walk through management's door for authority to make decisions. They should have been given the authority and power long ago. Management's primary job in the future is to be an internal "consultant" who helps to facilitate the change process. Figure 1-2 shows the evolution of this process.

One of management's primary jobs as a change agent will be to implement the Cycle Time Management process. A coordinated effort of this nature is essential to making Cycle Time Management work in your company. By its very nature, Cycle Time Management cannot be a one-shot program. It is a process, not an event. It is designed to look for more opportunities once it has solved the ones under consideration. Nor can Cycle Time Management work effectively if it is viewed as either a management-only program or a program that management starts and then forgets. This brings up another critical role for management in making Cycle Time Management work.

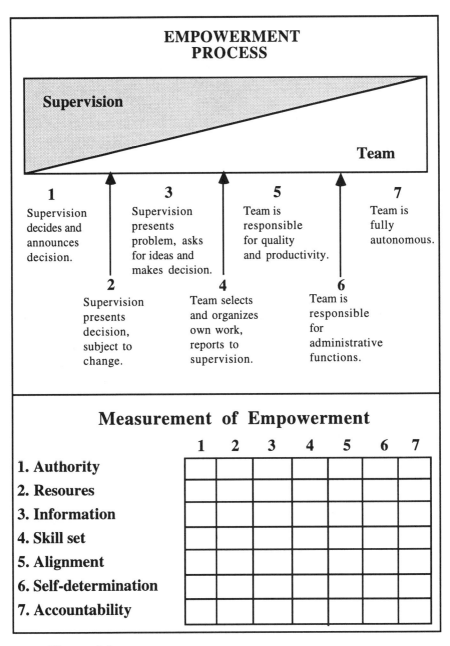

**EMPOWERMENT PROCESS**

Supervision

Team

**1**
Supervision decides and announces decision.

**3**
Supervision presents problem, asks for ideas and makes decision.

**5**
Team is responsible for quality and productivity.

**7**
Team is fully autonomous.

**2**
Supervision presents decision, subject to change.

**4**
Team selects and organizes own work, reports to supervision.

**6**
Team is responsible for administrative functions.

**Measurement of Empowerment**

|  | 1 | 2 | 3 | 4 | 5 | 6 | 7 |
|---|---|---|---|---|---|---|---|
| 1. Authority |  |  |  |  |  |  |  |
| 2. Resoures |  |  |  |  |  |  |  |
| 3. Information |  |  |  |  |  |  |  |
| 4. Skill set |  |  |  |  |  |  |  |
| 5. Alignment |  |  |  |  |  |  |  |
| 6. Self-determination |  |  |  |  |  |  |  |
| 7. Accountability |  |  |  |  |  |  |  |

Figure 1-2.

# Reengineering through Cycle Time Management

There must be more than just the verbal commitment of management to Cycle Time Management. Top management must be a fully participating member of the company's effort. Management must realize that they are a service department within the company. Their role is to be in constant communication with all the other functions in a company in order to provide the resources necessary to build a product or provide a service. To fulfill this role, management needs to have a clear vision of where the company is going. This vision must be driven by the marketplace in concert with the strategic plan. Above all, the company vision should make it clear that everybody in the company has the responsibility and authority to reduce cycle time. This is a must.

This is what the Levi Strauss company has done. In essence, their vision is the process of continuously seeking improvement. They don't wait until something breaks. Levi Strauss and companies who adopt Cycle Time Management are more like laboratories in which members of teams are constantly testing, analyzing and experimenting with new ways to eliminate waste and reduce cycle time. Levi Strauss is in the process of making every one of its 13,000 employees (as well as thousands more in foreign countries) into members of self-directed teams like the ones we mentioned earlier. The assignment for these teams is, in effect, to give the company a tune-up as it is driving down the highway. If that seems to be foolish or dangerous, consider that Levi Strauss in 1993 was already 7 percent ahead of 1992's figures for the first nine months of the fiscal year. In our opinion, they must be doing something right.

Changing spark plugs at sixty miles per hour doesn't have to be as difficult as it sounds, not when there is a systematic method for implementing Cycle Time Management. A company needs to work with the speed, accuracy and teamwork of a pit crew at the Indianapolis 500. The philosophy of waste and cycle time reduction is to bring cohesiveness, unity and integration into a company, not chaos. We have seen that this requires a culture change, a feedback cycle, and management commitment. These three core requirements are buttressed by a number of techniques which will vary to some degree with each individual company. The ones we list here are what we have found to be the most universal in our dealings with clients:

## CYCLE TIME MANAGEMENT TECHNIQUES

- **Establishment of "stretch" goals which require corporate-wide challenges and commitment.**

- **Cross-functional involvement in the strategic planning process including engineering, purchasing, planning, and manufacturing.**

- **Use of the team approach in process, product, and system development in order to maximize creative synergies.**

- **Establishment of "as-is" baselines and World Class measurements to monitor targeted against actual performance.**

- **Utilization of concurrency concepts and techniques in reaching product and organizational objectives.**

So far, we have defined core concepts and presented you with some lists, but we have not fully discussed what it will take to make Cycle Time Management work in your company. These concepts and lists form the foundation upon which two basic principles operate. These two principles can be summed up as:

**Uncovering obstacles,
and
Managing the "white spaces."**

What do we mean by these two concepts? The principle of uncovering obstacles is the same as the principle behind Just-In-Time. JIT said that if you lowered inventory levels, obstacles would appear which had been covered up by the excess inventory. Once the obstacles were uncovered, JIT practitioners did not see them as a problem, but as an opportunity to reduce or eliminate the original problem which had been covered up by wasteful activities. As you reduce cycle time, obstacles to the smooth functioning of your company will be revealed as you begin to eliminate wasteful activities. As with JIT, this should not be seen by your company as a problem, but as an opportunity to reduce cycle even further.

In their book, *Improving Performance: How to Manage the White Space on the Organization Chart*, Geary A. Rummler and Alan P.

## Reengineering through Cycle Time Management

Brache teach us a new way to look at organizations that fits in nicely with what we have to say about Cycle Time Management. Most of the obstacles, the disconnects, the bottlenecks in an organization are in the areas (the white spaces) between two departments or functions. Rummler and Brache describe these interfaces as "those points at which the baton (for example, 'production specs') is being passed from one point to another," as in a relay race during the Olympics. If you were to follow the "baton" through your company, you would see that it does not travel through the traditional structure of an organization with hierarchies of employees within segmented departments. Instead, the "baton" follows the flow of work which must be performed to build a product or provide a service to a customer. When they look at a company in this manner, Rummler and Brache see the organization as an adaptive system which operates at three levels — 1) The Organization Level, 2) The Process Level, and 3) The Job/Performer Level. In our experience, we have found that Rummler and Brache's hypotheses are almost always true. We have found that the successful implementation of Cycle Time Management must address all three levels.

We will be presenting a number of tools and techniques throughout this book which you can use in the implementation process, a process which in actuality never ends. There are three tools, however, that we do want to introduce at this point.

## Three Critical Tools

### WORLD CLASS ASSESSMENTS

Reducing cycle time and achieving status as a World Class company begins with the establishment of a baseline. We believe in this idea so strongly that we wrote a book about how to assess your company. *World Class: Measuring its Achievement* (PT Publications, West Palm Beach, FL) was written to assist companies so that they would not avoid taking this critically important and basic step in their rush to implement new business and management philosophies. The baseline is the mark from which a company will measure its progress.

Internal assessments will provide your company with a company-wide picture of your organization as well as a detailed picture of each function within the company. A company assessment that accurately evaluates where your company stands is the best way for you to stay competitive, even to survive, in a rapidly changing world.

Companies perform surveys, audits and assessments of themselves to determine their present status, where they have been and where they need to go in the future. Traditional methods of assessing a company's performance, however, no longer provide an accurate indication of an organization's viability and survivability. It stands to reason that a new philosophy of conducting business, Cycle Time Management, requires a new way of reviewing each company, a way which will reflect new process methods, practices and customer/supplier relations. In particular, this assessment needs to alert your company to:

1. **How much waste is present in company operations and related activities. Waste, today, is too often accepted as a given and absorbed into overhead costs. This is a reactive way of thinking and must change as we compete in the world market.**

2. **How actual performance compares to the stated goals and objectives. Observing this variance is instrumental in making new plans which will enable a company to take corrective action immediately.**

We strongly suggest that a steering group be formed to conduct an assessment or that outside assistance be utilized, instead of putting the burden solely on one department. Participants in the assessment are Customers (Major), Finance, Purchasing, Manufacturing, Engineering, Design, Sales, Marketing, Direct Labor and Suppliers. The World Class Assessment is a team effort taken to evaluate the internal and external aspects of a company. It is vital for the assessment team to be made up of individuals from a number of disciplines within a company. This is done so there will be input from a number of areas which will reflect the interconnected nature of your organization. It is also advisable to seek outside professional help to facilitate the assessment team since objectivity is crucial to the assessment's success and many people are protective of their own area this early in the process.

## WORLD CLASS MEASUREMENTS
Take a look at the various measurements gathered while

completing the assessment of your company. How many of your current measurements complement and interface with each other? How many measurements foster behavior which is essential to achieving a company's goals? For example, does Sales measure aggregate numbers while the factory measures line items to achieve the production schedule attainment? While Sales drives prices down, the ability to manage profits begins to erode. This is one example of the many measurement conflicts in companies today. We need to bring into synch all of the measurements used to drive cycle time reduction.

Companies must develop measurements that are interrelated and that focus on customer requirements instead of vague financial or market share considerations. The key, as we pointed out above, is to establish a baseline. Once a baseline is established, companies should measure and monitor their progress toward the achievement of World Class status. Equally important, measurements are useful as a dynamic management tool which establishes a results orientation in the workplace. Establishing meaningful measurements is a very difficult task and is somewhat unique to every organization. The measurements which follow are suggestions, ideas which have worked for many of our clients. But they worked only because the companies developed the measurements on their own. They would not have worked if we simply spoon-fed them to our clients. In the long run, your hard work in these early stages will pay off many times over.

## SUGGESTED CYCLE TIME OPPORTUNITIES

### Design Engineering
**Total Design Cycle Time**
**Number of Engineering Changes**
**Material Costs**
**Labor Costs (Direct and Indirect)**
**Production Cycle Time**
**Test Cycle Time**
**Components per Product**
**Component Standardization**
**Mean Time Between Failures**
**First Pass Drawing Accuracy**
**Number of Preproduction and Prototype Units Required**
**Bill of Material Levels**

## Manufacturing Engineering
**Manufactuability**
**Routing**
**Production Rates**
**Simplicity**
**Methodology**

## Sales Order Entry
**Order Entry Cycle Time**
**Order Entry Accuracy (Into and Out of Department)**
**Number of "Special" vs. Standard Orders**
**Number of Changes to Sales Orders**
**Number of Invoicing Problems Attributable to Order Entry**
**Number of Documents/Files Required**

## Purchasing
**Purchase Order Process Cycle Time**
**Requisition Errors**
**Requisition Approval Process**
**Purchase Order Errors**
**Number of Purchase Order Changes**
**Incoming Quality Levels from Suppliers**
**Incoming Count Accuracy from Suppliers**
**On-Time Delivery Rates from Suppliers**
**Supplier Lead Times**
**Number of Suppliers**

## Distribution
**Loss**
**Damage**
**Delays**
**Time**
**Data Entry Errors**
**Pick Accuracy**
**Load Utilization**

## Administration
**Unnecessary Reports**
**Unnecessary Delays**
**Errors**
**Equipment Downtime**
**Unnecessary Approvals**
**Batch Processing**

# Reengineering through Cycle Time Management

<u>Finance</u>
**Inaccurate Data**
**Incorrect Measurements**
**Closing Cycle Time**
**Journal Voucher Entries**
**Aging of Payables/Receivables**

## ACTIVITY BASED COSTING

Another critical tool is Activity Based Costing (ABC) which is a costing system that provides you with the information you need to run your company in the most efficient and profitable manner possible. ABC is a natural partner for all of the latest business philosophies. It works exceptionally well in conjunction with Just-In-Time, Supply Base Management, Total Quality Management, Agile Manufacturing, and, of course, Cycle Time Management. In fact, ABC is the link which brings all of these techniques together under a single financial umbrella.

Peter Grieco and Mel Pilachowski's book, *Activity Based Costing: The Key to World Class Performance* (PT Publications, West Palm Beach, FL), outlines the theory of ABC and shows you how to implement it at your company. As they were writing Activity Based Costing, Mel Pilachowski kept having the image of a weed-infested lawn in front of an otherwise neatly kept home. Every week, the owner would come out and mow down all the weeds. For about a day or so, the lawn looked pretty good. But after that, the weeds started popping up again all over the place.

In our minds, that is the state of costing in organizations today. We strongly believe the following are true:

- **Traditional accounting practices are weakening American business.**

- **The emphasis on financial measurements diverts us from improvement.**

- **Traditional cost systems hinder excellence by hiding the elements of cost.**

In other words, we mow down our problems every week and pretend that everything looks fine. And it does, for a couple of days. Then, those problems start popping up again all over the place.

22

Avoidance is not the answer when it comes to cost systems. If we do not search out the cost drivers in our companies and assign them directly to products and services, we are going to lose out in the global marketplace.

We must begin to use Activity Based Costing (ABC) as a tool to find the areas of opportunity in our organizations. It allows us to form a financial map of all accounting and finance areas. This is true whether we manufacture a product or provide a service. Our present way of assigning costs often makes problems worse.

## The First Steps for Your Company to Take

### STRATEGY

So far, we have provided you with an overview of Cycle Time Management and some of the tools you will need to make it a way of life in your company. No process of implementation is complete, however, without a strategy to guide it. The strategy for Cycle Time Management begins with a definition.

> **Total Cycle Time is the amount of time it takes to complete a task for an internal or external customer on time. It is neither the machine rate nor the ability to produce. It is not based on the employment rate and Total Cycle Time is not constant from month to month. Ideally, the Total Cycle Time is driven by this formula:**
> **DAILY SALES = DAILY RATE**

The strategy of Cycle Time Management must have two goals. One is to satisfy the customer by ensuring on-time delivery of quality products or services. Two is to use the Continuous Improvement Process to ensure the first goal, customer satisfaction. Although there will be a number of ways of achieving these goals, all methods will have the following common threads:

- **A focus on time as the key element.**

- **Commitment to reach objectives at all levels within the organization and across all functional boundaries.**

- **A team structure that builds synergy and maximizes the strengths of each participant.**

23

- **Investment of the required resources — time, money, materials, equipment and people.**

In upcoming chapters, we will look at the implementation and institutionalization processes in much more detail. But, to provide you with an idea of our approach, we offer the following guidelines which should be part of every strategic plan:

- **Assess your business and competition.**
- **Develop a mission/vision for your company.**
- **Determine how, when and why the planning process works.**
- **Determine and calculate risk factors.**
- **Get to be the best of class.**
- **Learn how to gather and use data.**
- **Develop a business plan that you can sell internally and externally.**
- **Organize and clarify your company's goals and objectives.**
- **Assign responsibility and authority to people.**
- **Identify major markets and segments.**
- **Conduct an internal assessment to be used as a reference point.**
- **Monitor the performance to plan.**
- **Conduct a financial evaluation and justification.**
- **Position your company effectively.**
- **Use cost objectives to influence the market.**

## RELATIONSHIP MAP

Once a company has a solid idea of what it wants to accomplish and how it is going to accomplish its mission, we advise companies to find out where they are standing. The first step in that task is to develop a Relationship Map. Earlier in this chapter, we discussed how Rummler and Brache in their book, *Improving Performance*, advised companies to look at the flow of work in their organizations rather than at departmental hierarchies. We think that this advice is what is needed to better manage cycle time. Rummler and Brache go on to define a Relationship Map as an illustration of "the inputs and outputs that flow among functions."

We have always told our clients to view the interfaces between divisions, between departments, between production lines, and

24

even between work stations as customer-supplier relationships. In other words, the principles of Supply Management should be as diligently applied to internal suppliers as they are to external ones. This is what, in essence, a Relationship Map makes graphic. As an example, we have developed a Relationship Map of the fictional Blackbox Company in Figure 1-3.

### PROCESS MAP
The next step in finding out where your company stands is to develop Process Maps which show how inputs are converted into outputs for any particular process. For example, a Process Map could show the exact sequence of steps taken by a company when it processes a customer return. Figure 1-4 shows a portion of this map for the Blackbox Company.

Process Maps can extend over a number of pages. Our example would probably cover six to seven pages in its complete form. In other words, a great deal of work will go into the development of Process Maps at your company. We recommend that this work be done by a team consisting of upstream suppliers, downstream customers, and personnel who actually perform the activities within the process. Furthermore, you should develop two Process Maps. One should be an "as-is" map which shows the baseline of current operations. The second map is then a "should-be" map. Corrective actions are the steps needed to turn the "as-is" condition into the "should-be" goal. We would like to note in the example above that the return authorization number would appear on the purchase order from the supplier. This in itself would be a cycle time reduction since it would eliminate the need for a telephone call after a defect occurs in order to obtain a return authorization.

### BENCHMARKING
The third step in establishing where your company stands is referred to as Benchmarking. Put simply, this is the seeking out of leading-edge practices used by best-in-class organizations. The plan is to emulate these practices in your own company in order to accelerate the progress toward World Class status. We will be discussing Benchmarking in more detail in the following chapters as it applies to specific activities within Cycle Time Management. Readers should also reference *The Benchmarking Book* by Michael J. Spendolini.

# Reengineering through Cycle Time Management

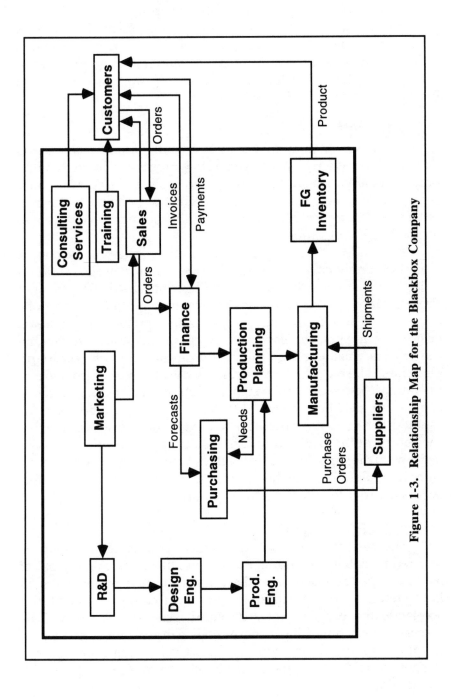

Figure 1-3. Relationship Map for the Blackbox Company

26

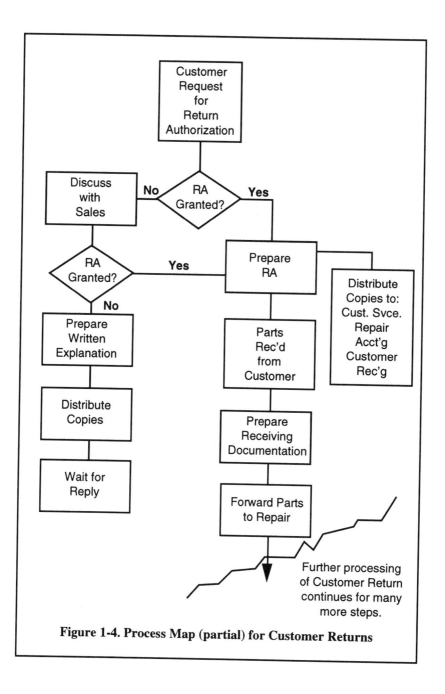

**Figure 1-4. Process Map (partial) for Customer Returns**

## Reengineering through Cycle Time Management

The preceding discussion centered around the first steps you will need to take in order to make Cycle Time Management into a cultural reality at your company. As we have mentioned, that transformation is not easy and requires at least two years of effort for it to become a way of life. We hasten to add, however, that you will begin noting some very favorable results much earlier. Speaking of early, that is where we will start the next chapter — early in the life cycle with the Design and Development Phase.

# Summary

### What is Cycle Time Management (CTM)?
Cycle Time Management is the integration of all the activities of an organization from customer need to customer satisfaction under one operating philosophy which seeks to build better products or provide better services faster than its competitors.

### Cycle Time Management's six-step cycle.
1) Calculate theoretical cycle time.
2) Gather data.
3) Analyze cycle components.
4) Begin problem solving.
5) Develop an action plan.
6) Institute measurement and feedback cycles.

### What is agile manufacturing and how does it relate to Cycle Time Management?
Agile manufacturing is an operative philosophy which seeks to respond precisely to customer wants. Like Cycle Time Management, agile manufacturing places an emphasis on zero inventory, zero waste, fast response times, and short production cycles.

### How will Cycle Time Management be institutionalized in an organization?
Three areas must be addressed in order for Cycle Time Management to be fully effective. They are:
- Culture change.
- Employee empowerment.
- Management commitment.

**What are some of the more critical tools needed to make Cycle Time Management work?**

Organizations which successfully make Cycle Time Management a way of life have learned and mastered the following tools:

- World Class assessments.
- World Class measurements.
- Activity Based Costing.
- Process mapping.
- Benchmarking World Class companies.
- Strategic planning.

# Action Steps

1) Develop a company strategy with the goals of (a) satisfying the customer by ensuring on-time delivery of quality products or services and (b) employing the Continuous Improvement Process to meet the first goal.

2) Draw up a Relationship Map of your company to help you understand the flow of work in your organization. Pay attention to the "white spaces," those places where departments or functions interface.

3) Draw up Process Maps to show how inputs are converted into outputs for any particular process designated by the Relationship Map.

4) Begin a Benchmarking program whereby you will emulate the best practices of the best-run organizations.

5) Start a Training and Education program immediately for Cycle Time Management and related topics. Suggestions for related areas would be Supply Management, Set-Up Reduction, Activity Based Costing, Team Building, Total Quality Management, etc.

# Chapter Two: Reducing the Design and Development Cycle

Because the Blackbox Company occupies a comfortable and protected niche in the electronics industry and because its designs and quality levels are superior, the company has experienced very few troublesome times in its history. But the company has not gone unnoticed. Several competitors have almost beaten them to the punch on a few blackbox products and only the company's sterling reputation kept customers from defecting. Surprisingly, the biggest scare came from a small $5 million dollar firm in New England. There were rumors in the industry that they were designing and developing a "sixth-generation" blackbox that would increase the capacity of earlier versions by 40% and could be produced for 15% less cost than standard models. The New England company was also attaining Six Sigma performance levels in the product's MTBF (Mean Time Between Failure) measurement. Fortunately, for the Blackbox Company, this upstart firm ran out of money. The latest rumors were that the company was now on the auction block.

## Reengineering through Cycle Time Management

How many times, Mary Andrews, Blackbox's president, wondered, can we dodge bullets like that? How come our "sixth-generation" blackbox is still two years away from production? Why are we missing schedules, and why is our cycle time for development so long?

"We are ahead of everybody else in the industry when it comes to this 'sixth-generation'," Andrews told us, "but that's not good enough. You and I both know that somebody out there is looking for venture capital right now to develop their latest design or buy out our competitors to introduce their own new products."

We couldn't agree more with her assessment. As the first step in our problem-solving venture with her company, we looked over the company's Relationship Map (see Figure 1-3; page 26). After a quick study, we immediately noticed two blatant disconnects, or white spaces. Both the Application Consulting Services and the Education departments were not providing data to anybody else in the company. As you may remember, Application Consulting Services helps customers determine new applications within their own companies for blackboxes. Education's role, as the name demonstrates, is to educate customers in the use of products and services.

We noticed that there was also a serious disconnect between suppliers and the Design and Development function. In other words, both ends of the business cycle were not being represented in the early design and development phases. Valuable information on the reliability of blackboxes in the field concerning failures and modifications were not being communicated back to the engineers and designers. The same lack of feedback was also true about the purchasing of new materials or circuits. Marketing talked to the Design and Development function, but their information exchange was chiefly focused on sales data and product placement. An important opportunity to cut total cycle time was being lost.

Next, we conducted a Process Mapping exercise with the Design and Development function. The most glaring deficiency was the acceptance of the myth that you can't cut the cycle time of creative people doing their jobs. Consequently, there were few measurements in place which tracked a new product's progress or success ratio. What we saw at a first glance, however, was that a good 50% of all the time spent in Design and Development was devoted to either redesign activities, repetitive paperwork or administrative activities. We knew that we could overcome cultural myths about creative people in a short time by creating an environment for engineers and designers which would allocate time for them to do what they truly enjoy — designing state-of-the-art products and processes.

# Benefits of Reducing Design and Development Cycle Time

What is the importance of cycle time to the design and development process? When you cut the time it takes to conceptualize, design and develop a new product or service in half, you gain an opportunity to gain market share, create a leadership role in the industry and enjoy the benefits of excellent product positioning. You also have the ability to double the number of new products or services that you introduce into the marketplace. This allows your company to reduce cost and to outmaneuver slower competition. You also beat the competition because early introduction of new products provides your sales force with more time to sell product.

In this chapter, we are going to illustrate how you can reduce the design and development cycle. For the most part, the techniques we will introduce either remove obstacles to the work flow or institute feedback loops. None of these techniques is particularly new, but the way they have been put together is innovative. One of the classic examples of a company with a remarkable design and development cycle is the Japanese bicycle manufacturer, National Bicycle Industrial Company. This small company assembles custom-made bicycles by hand, one bicycle at a time. In essence, they have lot sizes of one and a completely flexible manufacturing process. It is so flexible that customers are able to choose from 11,232,862 configurations. Even with that much variety, the design and development phase takes about as much time as it takes to enter color patterns, model type and customer sizes into the computer.

This computer, via a configuration module, generates a blueprint and a bar code label which travels with the bike-in-process. The bar code contains welding and painting information. What we found amusing and instructive about this example was that, although you had to wait two weeks for delivery, your bicycle is made in about three hours or less. The reason you have to wait so long? The company wants you to "feel excited about waiting for something special."

# Stages of Design
# and Development — Traditional

The example we have just described is the result of a new way of conducting design and development. Before we look at this new methodology in more detail, let's review the traditional methodology with an eye to where problems arise. The design and development phase begins with the identification of a customer's requirements and ends with the formulation of a production plan based on total cost and a design which is producible. For many companies, design and development is recognized as the most critical phase of the whole business cycle. We have often compared this phase to the preparation of healthy soil in a well-managed garden. The good gardener knows that tasty vegetables and full-blossomed flowers will be the result of careful design and development.

In the traditional design and development phase, a company familiarizes itself with its competition and the needs of its customers. It then begins to brainstorm for possible ways to satisfy customers or to produce products in a market opened up by the competition. The design for this new product (and it could just as well be the design of a new service) is then further developed and eventually a prototype is made. Those products which are found to satisfy specific customer requirements and meet reliability levels are then passed on to the manufacturing department.

The manufacturing department begins to define the process by which the product will be made. Tooling and fixturing are designed. A cost analysis and feasibility study is performed and, if passed, production scheduling begins. At this point, the traditional design and development function calls for procurement of any material or tooling needed to build the product. Since soft tooling is normally used in this stage, some companies never proceed to hard tool the product. Manufacturing then initiates a "prove-out" phase in which the manufacturing process is tested and refined. Once this process has been established, a quality plan is developed which is followed by a service support plan.

Then, it is time for the company to go into production and distribute the new product. The biggest question which arises after this lengthy process is whether the market for the new product still exists. A lot of time has probably gone by since that initial familiarization stage. Another question that comes up is whether the cost/ price ratio established earlier in the cycle is still viable. And, finally, what has the competition been doing during the time you were designing and developing the new product? You can be sure that they haven't been standing still. If you're lucky, you have a few months before they introduce a new product. If you're not, they introduced their new product about halfway through your cycle, so that you're left developing a product that is now obsolete.

To compound the time problem described above, management often gets involved too late in the cycle to exert any real influence. Figure 2-1 shows that just as management typically gets involved, their ability to change or redirect the design and development cycle becomes more difficult and extremely costly. It can sometimes feel like trying to stop a freight train to change direction in this traditional design cycle.

# Stages of Design and Development — Simultaneous Methodology

There is no logical reason why all the stages outlined in traditional design and development cycle have to be done one after the another. Many can be done concurrently. This not only cuts time out of the cycle, but often creates a synergy as different areas of a company are required to work together. It is this synergy which leads to higher quality products at reduced costs even though less time is taken. The table that follows (see Figure 2-2) shows the four stages of the new design and development cycle and the activities which are undertaken concurrently during each stage.

One of the major reasons why concurrent engineering is not conducted in the early design stages is that companies don't want to spend their dollars on two or three variations of product development. They would rather bet the ranch on one design and reengineer the product over and over. From an initial budget position, the "one-design" method appears less costly since development and overrides can be hidden and not reported. In the long run, however, the model we are proposing here is much less costly since it greatly reduces cycle time.

When we look at management's involvement and influence in the new design and development cycle (see Figure 2-3), we see that

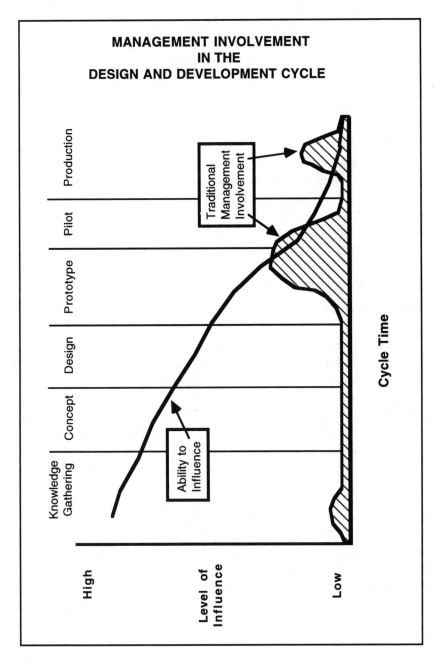

Figure 2-1. Management Involvement in the Design and Development Cycle — Traditional

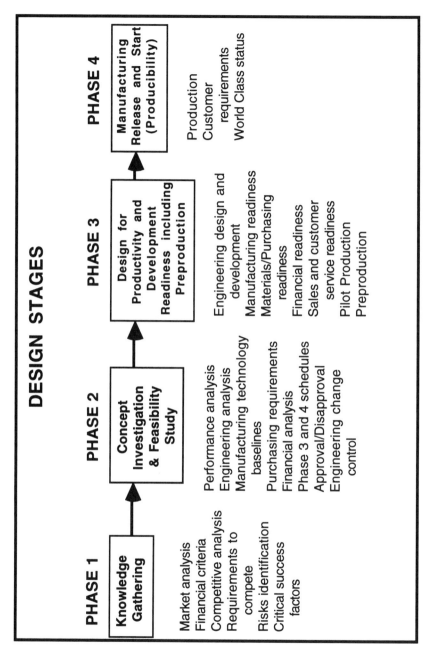

Figure 2-2. Design and Development Stages

## Reengineering through Cycle Time Management

management and suppliers are involved at precisely those times when they have the greatest ability to influence costs and design considerations. This is the opposite of what we found in the traditional cycle (see Figure 2-1).

This is made even more clear in Figure 2-4 and Figure 2-5. Both charts show when problems typically arise for each methodology. Problems which occur late in the cycle (that is, to the right of the chart) cost more money and take more resources to correct. Conversely, problems which occur early in the design and development cycle (to the left of the chart) are far easier and less costly to correct. As the charts show, the simultaneous methodology is more responsive and less costly.

The simultaneous methodology attempts to overcome a mindset which only sees activities as sequential events. One of the first tasks that you will undertake as you institute a simultaneous methodology is to establish teams that work on one product from beginning to end. An engineer working in this type of team environment can concentrate his or her knowledge on each new product or process being developed. Breaking up the old monolithic approach allows teams to begin overlapping activities. As a task becomes more manageable, we have found that communication increases between cross-functional people in each team and throughout the company. And we have found that when communication increases, it is just a matter of time before quality begins to improve and costs begin to shrink.

# Concurrent Engineering and Cycle Time Management

### CONCURRENT ENGINEERING

**The creation of an environment in which all functional disciplines that contribute to the design, development, production, distribution, and sale of a product or service perform their functions concurrently and cooperatively versus sequentially.**

Concurrent engineering is fundamental to the effort to reduce the time to market of new products and services or enhancements to existing offerings. Also known as concurrency, it focuses attention on the concept and design stages where the impact of a change is least

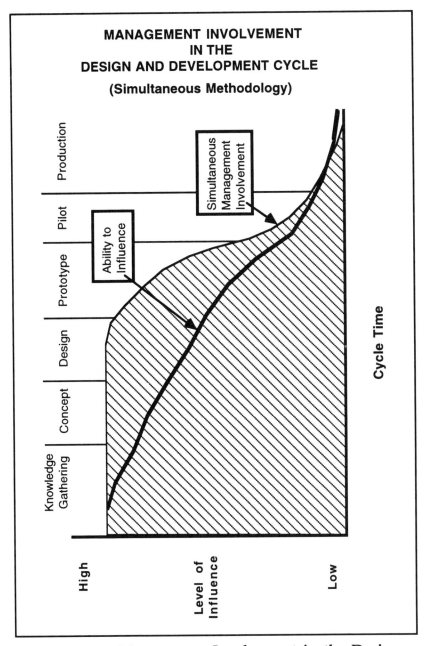

Figure 2-3. Management Involvement in the Design and
Development Cycle — Simultaneous Methodology

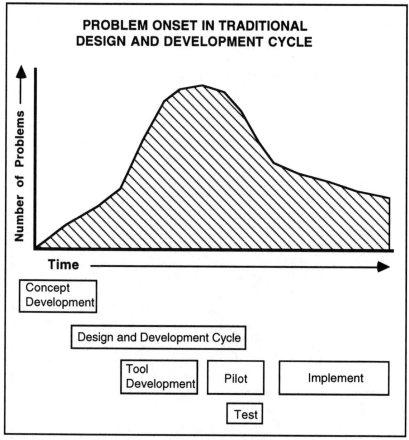

Figure 2-4. Problem Onset in Traditional Cycle

costly and least likely to adversely affect reaching the market on time. Quality is designed into the product and the process at the same time, thus guaranteeing that the product is producible and conforms to customer requirements. There are a number of principles and techniques which are gathered under the "concurrent" umbrella. Another book would be required to cover the entire subject and give it justice. We will describe a few of the more important concepts here.

**Design**
**Standardization**
- **Use existing components whenever possible**
- **Use similar designs as basis for new components**

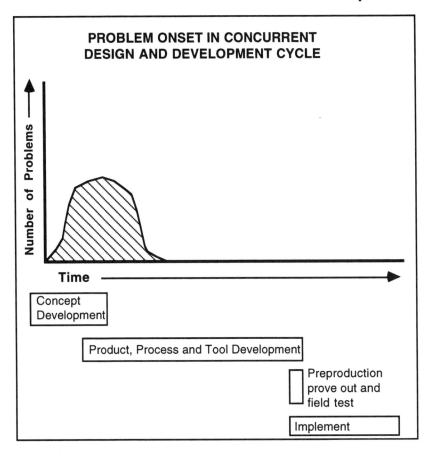

Figure 2-5. Problem Onset in Simultaneous Cycle

- **Establish policy and rules of design**
- **Standardize tools**

**Design of
Experiments
(Taguchi, Shainin,
Classical)**
- **Reduce and control variation in process and product**
- **Design out potential nonconformances**
- **Identify critical parameters affecting product and process performance**
- **Predict product performance levels**

# Reengineering through Cycle Time Management

Quality Function
Deployment
- Translate customer requirements into technical requirements for each stage in the product/process development cycle
- Ensure that product/process objectives are maintained throughout the development cycle
- Ensure that marketing strategy stays intact during transition from concept to final product
- Ensure that manufacturing control points are identified and maintained
- Maintain common focus, purpose and priorities

Process Control
Planning
- Identify actions required at each stage of process in order to ensure conformance using statistical methods
- Identify sources of variation for every operation in the process
- Evaluate the viability of measurement systems used in the process
- Identify relationships between product requirements and process capabilities

Simulation
Techniques
- Evaluate product and process characteristics concurrently to determine the optimum product and process designs
- Identify successful simulations and models

Group Technology
- Produce small lots to increase run time between set-ups
- Identify similar processes on similar machine tools
- Build in speed and flexibility

Value
Engineering
- Use to increase performance to required form, fit and function specifications at the lowest total cost
- Identify white spaces and nonvalue-added activities

**Design for
Producibility
and Assembly**
- **Maximize, through design, the inherent characteristics of a product, system, process or component configuration to ensure the most efficient and economical method of fabrication, assembly, inspection, test, maintenance, installation, and final acceptance. (More on this later in the chapter.)**

**Synchronous
Manufacturing**
- **Use to maximize the acceleration of materials through the production process while minimizing resource utilization to minimize costs**

Be forewarned, however. Concurrent engineering is most effective when a combination of upstream and downstream functions work together in a team environment during the concept and design stages. The team should seek to isolate product and process problems and to eliminate them utilizing problem-solving tools. This approach will help the design and development function create better product and process designs. Companies are already reducing the time to introduce new products by 50-60%, combined with a 40-45% reduction in resource requirements. The following list demonstrates the key benefits that we have noted in our work with clients:

### KEY BENEFITS OF
### CONCURRENT ENGINEERING

- **Simultaneous design of products and processes**
- **Time savings**
- **Fewer design changes**
- **Reduction in the moving target syndrome**
- **Lower costs**
- **Early detection of problems**
- **Resource savings**
- **Cross-functional skills**
- **Improved communication**
- **Improved cooperation**
- **Early supplier involvement**
- **Technological advantages**

### Reengineering through Cycle Time Management

- **Process optimization**
- **Automated manufacturing capabilities**
- **Go/No-go decision timeliness**
- **Interdisciplinary creativity**
- **Destruction of barriers**

## CAD/CAM and Cycle Time Management

Let's look at an example of a company employing state-of-the-art CAD/CAM (Computer Aided Design/Computer Aided Manufacturing) techniques in a concurrent environment. *Industry Week* (April 19, 1993) recently ran an article about the use of CAD/CAM at the Ross Operating Valve Co. in Troy, Michigan. With the purchase of over $30 million worth of CAD systems and automated processing equipment, it is now possible for the company to work with customers in designing and producing customized valves, sometimes with delivery in three days.

The process begins with an engineer who is not only skilled in design, but in facets of manufacturing as well. This multiskilled engineer receives a call from a customer and, in a give-and-take session, designs the valve at his terminal. Later, he takes the valve design and designs the process for producing the product. All of this information is then downloaded into the CNC (Computer Numerically Controlled) machines on the production floor. And, three days later, the valve should be in the customer's hand.

Another valuable benefit of CAD/CAM production is that customer changes can be quickly incorporated into the design/process packet of information. In fact, the company envisions the day when the customer will be able to transmit changes by directly accessing Ross Operating Valve Co.'s computer terminals. Then, the Ross Co. will add its knowledge of pneumatic technology and send the revised design back to the customer. When a final design is approved, Ross Operating Valve will then build the product at the production site closest to the customer and ship the next day.

## Designing for Producibility

The Ross Operating Valve Co. is able to do what it does because it has overcome many of the obstacles which delay the design and production processes. Since each functional area in a company addresses its role differently in product development, we need to focus on how to interface those areas so as to eliminate delays and reduce the costs of development. The latest thrust in product development is aimed at realigning the organization and involving its parts in a company-wide effort. How to obtain this symbiotic relationship is the key to success.

Product and process design is done at the same time in order to ensure that the designed product can indeed be produced in the most cost-effective manner possible and with the highest quality and shortest set-up time.

The advantages of doing product and process design according to the DFP concept are as follows:

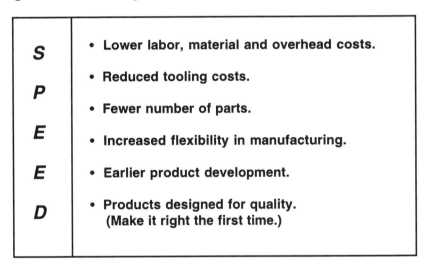

| S | • **Lower labor, material and overhead costs.** |
| P | • **Reduced tooling costs.** |
| E | • **Fewer number of parts.** |
| | • **Increased flexibility in manufacturing.** |
| E | • **Earlier product development.** |
| D | • **Products designed for quality.**<br>**(Make it right the first time.)** |

These advantages can be best achieved by setting objectives and developing strategies in which a product design team, consisting of people from engineering, manufacturing and from the suppliers of material or parts, resolves problems early in the design process.

## The Design for Producibility Team

The primary requirement in the design process is to establish product design teams and to train employees to use the rules below in developing a library of resources in order to come up with their own solutions to tooling, equipment, product and production problems. The purpose of the DFP team is to solve problems early in the design process before large amounts of money, time or other resources have been used or committed. This is where a Computer Aided Design (CAD) system comes into its own. CAD systems are designed to allow users to try "what if" solutions. A CAD system allows a company to ask questions like "What if we made the product from a different material?", "What if we changed this dimension?", etc. and see the repercussions of that decision. It can perform structural and mechanical analyses on products. A CAD system can connect the user to a database of drawings, specifications, bills of material, process sheets, inspection instructions, and so on. Sophisticated systems also support the concept of the virtual factory in which digitized information about design, routings, tooling, etc. can be sent to any production site in the world. This does not mean, of course, that a company is precluded from applying the design rules below if it does not have a CAD system.

- **Use fewer components or assemblies.**
- **Eliminate fasteners.**
- **Strive for simple designs.**
- **Design for testing, not inspection.**
- **Reduce complexity.**
- **Utilize the plug and play concept (modular design).**
- **Establish quick change technology.**
- **Employ the top-down assembly rule.**
- **Design for one surface processing.**
- **Minimize hidden pockets.**
- **Use snap together designs.**
- **Standardize components.**

The guiding principle behind all these rules and requirements of DFP is really very simple. The principle says that the best designed part or tool is no part or tool at all and that the best designed process is no process at all. In essence, this is a "zero-defect" philosophy for design. If a company designs a machine, process or product right the first time, it will make the product right the first time and every time.

# Early Involvement of Suppliers

One final note about Design for Producibility and Cycle Time

Management. We have often found that suggesting early involvement of suppliers as part of the design team shocks many companies
even though the material content of a product typically accounts for
60 to 80 percent of the cost. Why, then, should it be any surprise to
involve somebody responsible for such a large portion of product
cost? Especially when you consider that one of the reasons you chose
them as a supplier was for their level of expertise.

We have encountered companies where nobody has ever considered bringing in suppliers during the design stage. When we have
asked "Why?", they reply that the suppliers don't really know what
the company is going to need for its product. They forget that when
a supplier is selected, it should be because they are an expert in the
commodity being offered.

We reply that you shouldn't have selected them in the first
place unless you thought they had the capability. Suppliers are in a
position to play a role up front by providing visibility into your
design needs. We aren't saying that all suppliers will be that coopera-
tive and aggressive about solving your design problems, but the
majority will be if there is an incentive for them to help out. If they
can reduce your costs, you will be able to build more of the product
and subsequently they will get more business from you. Early
involvement of the supplier makes good business sense. Obviously,
selecting the right supplier is a prerequisite. Hence, supply management, which is noted in Chapter One, is a prime capability.

## Benchmarking — How to Hit a Moving Target

We have included a general discussion of benchmarking in this
chapter for two reasons. First, benchmarking can and should be used
to identify and emulate those companies who excel at design and
development techniques. Second, we consider benchmarking to be a
sound method for designing the strategic thrust of your company. In
essence, the use of benchmarking allows you to form or improve
upon your own company's methods of operation by taking certain
practices from Company X and another set of practices from Company Y and applying them. Benchmarking is intended to provide
opportunities to make breakthrough improvements in addition to
incremental improvements through the continuous improvement
process. What we want to accomplish is to learn from the best-in-
class on each element or phase in our own organization. We need to

be asking ourselves who are the world leaders.

The rationale behind benchmarking is that the competition in today's marketplace is evolving at an ever increasing rate. The static targets that you may have once used are no longer effective. New markets are opening and closing faster than many companies can follow. The only way to keep ahead is to leapfrog over the competition by identifying and emulating the leading-edge practices of companies who are best-in-class. This rarely means emulating the practices of an entire company. What you will be doing is studying the practices of one department or function of the benchmarked company and an entirely different department or function in another company. Look beyond you own industry for companies to benchmark. The idea is to use the best of the best in designing your own organization.

Like the Continuous Improvement Process, benchmarking is also a continuous process. You should always be searching for companies which are performing better than your company and conducting a comparison to see what can be learned. There is always some organization you can learn from and that company may be in an industry totally unrelated to your own. Who would have guessed that Xerox could learn so much from L.L. Bean?

What follows is a very brief outline of the activities constituting a benchmarking study. For a thorough discussion, we recommend reading *The Benchmarking Book* (Amacom, New York, NY) by Michael J. Spendolini, *The Benchmarking Workbook* (Productivity Press, Cambridge, MA) by Gregory H. Watson and *Benchmarking* (Quality Press, Milwaukee, WI) by Robert C. Camp.

## THE BENCHMARKING PROCESS

### 1) IDENTIFY THE AREA TO BE BENCHMARKED
- **Is the area selected as a result of the company's mission statement?**
- **Did you determine benchmark candidates based upon their critical importance to the company?**
- **Do the objectives of the benchmarking study include best practices and their corresponding metrics?**
- **Have operating and upper management, as well as key customers, been included in the discussion of benchmarking objectives?**

## 2) IDENTIFY THE CORRECT BENCHMARKING PARTNERS
- Have you selected benchmark partners based upon a unique functional excellence that you can apply in your company? Or for their general best-in-class recognition?

## 3) INFORMATION SOURCES
- Were all applicable sources of information on best-in-class practices researched?
  — Internal data?
  — Public information?
  — Site visits?
  — Supply base?
  — Customers?
  — National award winners?
  — National trade associations?
- Were all research methods reviewed for applicability prior to initiating research?

## 4) GAP ANALYSIS
- Did the research reveal key differences between the practices in your company and the benchmarked company?
- Did the research reveal why those differences exist?
- Did the research reveal how the benchmarked company obtained best-in-class results?
- Did the research indicate methods for closing the existing gap?

## 5) PLANNING
- Have strategic and tactical action plans been developed to address and close the gap?
- Are these action plans dynamic or static in design?

## 6) OBJECTIVE SETTING
- Have the gap and its corrective action plans been communicated to the affected parties for review and concurrence?
- Is there commitment within the affected functions and at the senior management level to implement these action plans?

## 7) IMPLEMENTATION
- Do the corrective action plans clearly define the steps

required by all parties to implement the required
changes, including time targets and metrics?
- **Has the plan been effectively implemented?**
- **Are monitoring techniques in place and in use?**
- **Is the plan recalibrated as required to ensure
effectiveness and continuous improvement?**
- **Has the benchmarking concept become part of the
culture of your organization?**

# Some Solutions to Problems in the Design and Development Cycle

We began this chapter with a set of problems. Now we are
going to briefly show you how we would have addressed the
problems at the hypothetical Blackbox Company. As you may
remember, one of the most blatant disconnects was the fact that two
departments critical to design and development were isolated from
the rest of the company. Our first suggestion was that the company
initiate a Design for Producibility team. We pointed out that the two
isolated departments, Application Consulting Services and Training, should be on the team. Application Consulting Services, which
helped customers find new applications for blackboxes, would be
instrumental in identifying new areas to develop. We were certain
that their input would help move the Blackbox Company even closer
to the leading edge. Training would be equally instrumental in the
design and development phase for their ability to show the company
what was working and what wasn't. The reason why customers had
any difficulty learning how to operate a blackbox was usually a
design problem.

The president quickly put our suggestions to work. She suggested that we add two major suppliers on the team and we quickly
agreed. It was going to be our next suggestion. We had seen too many
other examples of companies missing opportunities because they
had not tapped the expertise of their suppliers.

Now that we had the design and development cycle covered
from supplier to customer, we turned our attention to the department itself. It was a very good one. There was definite administrative
waste, but we had no doubt that Andrews and her staff could get rid
of it. We decided to suggest to Andrews that she take advantage of

the department's good operating condition and start a benchmarking study of the design departments of other companies to find ways to improve even further. Good as the department was, we were certain they could identify better practices by turning their formidable research skills on the process of design itself. As it turned out, several lower-level managers had begun informal benchmarking studies of their own, and they soon became company-wide champions. But we were not finished. Andrews wanted us to take a look at the manufacturing side next. She was certain we could cut some more cycle time there.

## Summary

### Why reduce design and development cycle time?

By cutting the time it takes to design and develop a new product or service in half, you can double the number of new products or services that you introduce into the marketplace. This makes your company more diversified and competitive.

### Why is the simultaneous methodology for design and development superior to the traditional methodology?

Since there is no reason why some stages in the traditional design and development cycle cannot be done at the same time, there is an immediate cut in cycle time by doing them simultaneously. This allows a company to change designs earlier in the process at a substantial savings in resources and time.

### What is concurrent engineering?

Concurrent engineering is an environment in which all functional disciplines contribute to design, development, production, distribution and sale of a product or service. The company performs these activities concurrently and cooperatively instead of sequentially. Quality is designed into the product and process at the same time, thus guaranteeing that product is producible and conforms to customer requirements.

### What is the principle behind Designing for Producibility?

The guiding principle says that the best designed part and tool is no part or tool at all and that the best designed process is no process at all.

## Reengineering through Cycle Time Management

**What is benchmarking?**

Benchmarking is the continuous study of other companies and their departments to identify practices which can improve operations in your own company. Once a best-of-the-best practice is identified, your company should find out how to emulate and adapt the practice in your own company.

# Action Steps

1) Explore ways in which you can use a simultaneous methodology in your company's design and development cycle.

2) Institute concurrent engineering. Begin with educational seminars and workshops. Define ways in which your company can design the product and the process for manufacturing the product at the same time. Go over the ideas outlined on pages 38 to 43.

3) If you are not using CAD/CAM, investigate how it could be used at your company. If you are using CAD/CAM, determine if you are using the system to its fullest capacity. Remember that computerization or automation is only effective when the underlying operations are logical and sound. Computerizing chaos just leaves you with computerized chaos.

4) Immediately form a Designing for Producibility team. Include suppliers on the team as well as personnel from engineering, manufacturing, marketing, and finance.

5) Begin a pilot benchmarking study. It does not have to be in the design and development area, but your first effort should be of a manageable size. Most importantly, it should be an area where you can get an immediate payback.

# Chapter Three: Manufacturing Technology

We arrived at the Blackbox Company early Monday morning about a half-hour before our scheduled meeting with its president and Manufacturing staff. We arrived early with the first shift of factory workers. Not wanting to wait for a coffee at the meeting, we asked a couple of the workers where we could get a cup. They told us there was a coffee machine on the factory floor. We thanked them and stepped into the factory itself.

A factory floor before workers arrive is a quiet place, but a very revealing one. We decided to take the long route to the coffee machine and gather some information. The first thing we noticed was large queues of inventory at the beginning and end of each step in the process. In between, the levels of stock varied from very small to medium-sized quantities; certainly not lot sizes of one. This suggested two basic problems to us: 1) The lines were not in balance, and 2) Inventory management was in need of improvement.

Near the coffee machine, there were a couple of workstations and, as we sipped our coffee and tea, we wandered over to them to see what we could learn. What we discovered was that there was no evidence of any statistical charts. We made a note to discuss the extent of the company's use of Statistical Process Control. What we saw next was not so surprising. A set-up team of two workers was readying one of the workstations for today's production. When we asked them why they were here before everybody else, they replied that they always came four hours early on change-over days or stayed late the day before in order to have the machines ready to run when the first shift came in. Clearly, this signaled an opportunity for improvement in the set-up reduction area as well.

While talking to this team, we also asked them how worn the machine tools were that they were positioning on the machine. "Pretty old," one of the workers said. "How worn was 'pretty old'?" we wanted to know. The worker was a veteran. He picked up the tool and held it to the light. "This one is on its last job. I can tell by the wear. It's a good thing you asked the question. This one's about ready to go. I'll have to get a new one."

We thanked him and commented on how knowledgeable he was, but we were bothered by the company's lack of a structured Preventive Maintenance program. The worker said he had heard of some companies who replace parts and tools before they break. That made sense to him. And to us. We had a pretty good idea of who we would suggest to be on a Preventive Maintenance team.

We finished our coffee and tea and went upstairs to the meeting. Our little tour had provided us with a lot to talk about.

# Cycle Time Management and Understanding Manufacturing Technologies

In the area of manufacturing, a company today must understand all of the new technologies which have become prominent in the past decade. By technology, we mean more than machines. We mean any tool or method which allows a company to build products or provide services of guaranteed quality at increased rates and lower costs. In this chapter, we will focus on a number of manufacturing technologies which will help your company reduce cycle time. One factor that all of these innovations have in common is the recognition that manufacturing is not an island upon which only traditional manufacturing activities are practiced. As you begin to study cycle time, it becomes readily apparent that companies need to look at how manufacturing interfaces with logistics, transportation, procurement, lead time reduction and supply base management. The time has come to link manufacturing activities with customer- and supplier-related activities in an effort to create a synergistic system that drives waste out of the manufacturing area of your company.

Furthermore, as we noted in Chapter One, the world of manufacturing is moving away from mass production to the production of highly customized products. This agile manufacturing paradigm will put an emphasis on the ability to reconfigure production processes. Machines and production lines must be designed to be modular and flexible. The effort should be to reduce cycle time to the lowest level possible by designing both the product and associated production processes at the same time.

## Cycle Time Management and the Paradigm Shift in Manufacturing

What we are experiencing today is a paradigm shift from the lean and flexible styles exemplified by Just-In-Time and Total Quality Control to a more inclusive style which emphasizes the operations of the entire company and not just the factory floor. We have summarized these shifts in Figure 3-1 on pages 56 and 57.

As the Figure 3-1 shows, companies are moving toward becoming teams of production generalists who are ready to reconfigure their core competencies for the production of a product which will satisfy a niche demand. What this means for manufacturing is that they will need to identify problems and opportunities on the production floor so that they can use new technologies to cut cycle time.

Now that you understand the goals of Cycle Time Management, we are ready to present the manufacturing technologies which will help you reduce cycle time. Which technologies and methods you select to use will be based on your company's present condition and future needs. Read over the following descriptions and decide on the combination which will work best in your organization.

## Effects of Group Technology, Cellular Operations and Process Flow on Cycle Time Management

The reduction of manufacturing cycle time should start with a process mapping of the plant and its operational flow. A process map will reveal the time involved in completing each operation and activity in the manufacturing cycle. The next step is to organize an improvement team to analyze each operation and activity to determine which are value-added and which are nonvalue-added. The

# AGILE MANUFACTURING

## *The Paradigm Shift*

| Lean/Flexible Model | Cycle Time Management Model |
|---|---|
| • Eliminate inventory | • Zero inventory |
| • Eliminate waste | • Zero waste |
| • Flexibility in scheduling | • Build to sales — daily |
| • Shortened lead times | • Minimum lead times |
| • Six Sigma quality in products and services | • Quality & reliability measured in terms of total life cycle costs |
| • Low unit cost via large volumes of similar products | • Low unit costs from:<br>  - Modular production facilities<br>  - Easily programmable equipment<br>  - Enterprise integrated information systems |
| | • Virtual products for each customer |
| • Focus is on factory floor enhancement of thru-put | • Focus is on total enterprise cycle time |
| • Task-oriented training of employees | • Enterprise-based training of employees for maximum capability and creativity |
| • Equipment & technology as primary asset | • Employees as primary asset |
| • Effective use of resources to contain costs | • Social responsibility<br>  - Products designed for recyclability and reconfigurability<br>  - Design-focused product changeover capability |

**Figure 3-1. (Part 1) Manufacturing's Paradigm Shift**

| AGILE MANUFACTURING | |
|---|---|
| *The Paradigm Shift* | |
| **Lean/Flexible Model** | **Cycle Time Management Model** |
| • Clearly defined roles<br>  - Customers<br>  - Competitors<br>  - Suppliers<br>  - Manufacturers/providers<br>  - Stakeholders | • Constantly changing roles as<br>  defined by the requirements<br>  of the virtual enterprise |
| • Broad-based market view:<br>  economies of scale | • Economies of scope: focus on<br>  servicing ever smaller niches |
| • Fragile to the impact of change:<br>  optimized for one purpose<br>  - Focused factory | • Change optimized:<br>  - Equipment<br>  - People<br>  - Information systems<br>  - Equipment<br>  - Supply base<br>  - Admin. systems & structures<br>  - Technologies |
| • Product designs are rigid and<br>  "frozen" only after numerous<br>  changes and enhancements<br>  - Value-added approach | • Products are designed for:<br>  - Producibility<br>  - Maintainability<br>  - Disassembly<br>  - Reconfigurability<br>  - Upgradability<br>  - Recyclability |
| • Products are designed for<br>  internal integration | • Products designed for<br>  maximum cycle time<br>  effectiveness |
| • Operationally focused:<br>  - Short-term financial<br>  - Extend status quo as long as<br>    possible to amortize costs | • Strategically focused:<br>  - Long-term performance<br>  - Diffused authority<br>  - Dynamic corporate structure |

**Figure 3-1. (Part 2) Manufacturing's Paradigm Shift**

# Reengineering through Cycle Time Management

Japanese, for example, stress that all motion, or movement of material, subassemblies or products, is waste and thus a nonvalue-added cost. Thus, the improvement team should be considering ways to reduce or eliminate nonvalue-added activities such as product movement and wait time. Another task for the improvement team is to analyze why inventory levels exist in queue, movement and staging. This is material not being worked on and should be assigned a cost.

We saw the steps suggested above put into action by one of our clients, Hat Brands, Inc., the manufacturers of Stetson and Resistol western hats. The business had been set up in a traditional manner, but when Bob Stec came on board as the new president and CEO, he wanted to introduce speed and flexibility into the company. Bob wanted cellular manufacturing throughout all of the divisions. Ken Paulk, the vice president of operations, tackled cloth hat manufacturing (golf and baseball hats) in Virginia. Pete Grieco, Pro-Tech's president and CEO, took on western hats in Texas. And Joe Becker, director of engineering, addressed felt production issues.

First, the process was mapped and a team was formed to lay out the factory in a Zone Concept (as shown in Figure 3-2) with small cells supporting the zone. A team was then given the following guidelines on cell design:

## CELL DESIGN CHARACTERISTICS

To facilitate the team in the process of cell design, we have formulated the following list of characteristics of an effective and efficient cell structure. These characteristics should be viewed as baseline benchmarks against which we measure suggestions and ideas. Those ideas which don't promote or advance one or more of the characteristics should not be included in the cell structure.

- **Structure should be process oriented — Identify the commonalities between each process in order to simplify the overall process.**

- **Minimize cycle time — Reduce cycle time between and within each process. Think in terms of hours rather than days.**

- **Minimize the distance or connection between each**

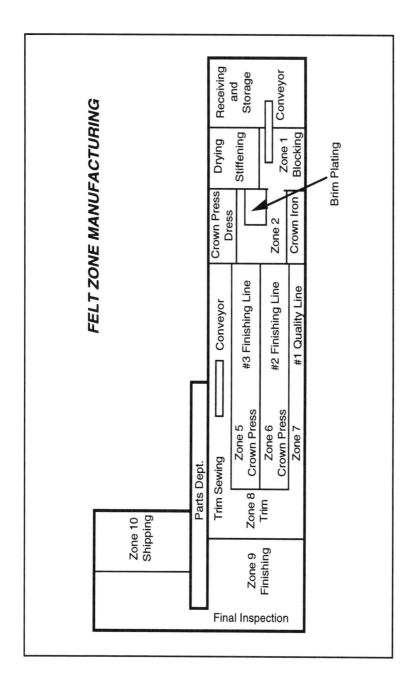

Figure 3-2. Felt Zone Concept

process point — Consider any staging or batching as a constraint to this minimal distance and flow concept. Minimize material handling.

- Make the work flow in one direction only — Rework, or reprocessing, is counterproductive. No reverses.

- Maximize flexibility — A borderless environment with borderless people. Focus attention on multi-skilled people and structural designs that are modular in concept and flow.

- Design for minimum number of steps — Find balance between simple steps and number of steps. Your guideline should be for a step to avoid a bottleneck and add value to the process.

- Consider the personnel skill level needed and the training required — personnel must be flexible and adaptable. Training must provide consistency and a way to measure for minimizing error.

The team quickly determined that a major cycle time delay resulted from the drying of hat bodies which, in most cases, took 72 hours to dry. With the aid of Mel Pilachowski, vice president of Pro-Tech, the group developed an oven that could dry hats in 12 minutes. This entailed buying custom-designed infrared ovens with a Programmable Logic Controller (PLC). The PLC was included in the oven's control systems to provide maximum flexibility for the oven's operation.

The primary job of an improvement team is to challenge every inefficiency in the process and to search for value-added solutions. Part of this brainstorming and problem-solving activity requires the team to familiarize itself with new technologies which can help the company not only solve problems, but become a world leader in the product or service provided. When improvement teams are exposed to proper training and given the time to put their analysis tools to work, the results are sometimes astounding.

At Neodata, which manages invoicing and subscriptions for national magazines, we did work with a team that produced the following achievements in the fulfillment management area:

## UPDATE PATCHES
Created a log of all update patches. Reviewed for completeness and accuracy. Can be used as a reference guide to special processing requested by clients.
**Benefit:** Outdated patches were deleted, resulting in faster problem resolution.

## REWORK STATS
Rework is now reported daily rather than weekly or monthly.
**Benefit:** Errors can be analyzed and fixed immediately. Reduced amount of rework going forward.

## REPORT RELEASE
Checklist created to ensure proper reports are printed and routed to clients and internal personnel.
**Benefit:** More timely receipt of reports; accurate distribution.

## FILE CONSOLIDATION
Duplicate hardcopy files have been consolidated throughout the customer service center. Duplicate files have been eliminated now that departments can share the files and have proximity to the required information.
**Benefit:** Saves filing time and space; faster access to information.

## UPDATE BALANCING
Accelerated balancing schedule instituted for updates.
**Benefit:** Accelerated processing in lettershop now that jobs are balanced sooner. Jobs can be printed earlier in the day.

## CLIENT INSTRUCTION SCHEDULE
Receipt of client instructions for update and label coding is tracked on an online system.
**Benefit:** There is an improved opportunity to work with clients on late instructions. Delays in updates and lettershop processing are reduced. Rework and overtime have been reduced in completing control programs.

## CIRCULATION ACCOUNTING
Circulation accounting clerk is now located in the customer service center and kept informed of all rework and reports printed. Reports are printed in the same location for quick access and balancing.
**Benefit:** Time delay and transportation expense due to printing in

# Reengineering through Cycle Time Management

one location and trucking to location of the circulation accounting clerk has been eliminated.

The list above is only half of the work going in on this area to reduce cycle time. The Neodata team is currently working on these other opportunities in the fulfillment management area:

### LABEL INSTRUCTIONS UPLOAD
Label instructions will be uploaded from a diskette provided by client.
**Benefit:** Reduce labor and keying errors.

### ZERO COUNT JOBS
Hundreds of job envelopes are created monthly with zero counts. Efforts are underway to suppress the creation of these job envelopes and to reduce the amount of stock that is blank in a print run.
**Benefit:** Decrease stock spoilage. Reduced cost of job envelopes and reduced labor to handle.

### SPECIAL JOB TRACKING
Special jobs are being placed on the local area network. Procedures are being developed to track and ensure that special jobs are being billed to clients.
**Benefit:** Quick reference for pricing information and assurance of immediate billing after job is completed.

### METER ROOM
Manual process has been updated. A download from personal computers to Finance and Accounting ensures more timely and accurate postage accounting billing. The Balancers and Meter Room Operator functions have been combined.
**Benefit:** Reduced headcount by two per customer service center.

### INSERTER LAYOUT
Testing is in progress on various insert machine configurations to increase productivity.
**Benefit:** Decreased headcount.

### PRODUCTIVITY GOALS
Specific productivity and performance goals are being established. There is an increased awareness of standards and measurements against standard.
**Benefit:** Improved productivity.

Another client, Heileman Brewing, also has worked hard on improving the operational flow of their packaging department. To show the difficulty of their job, we have included the "before" process map of their packaging flow in Figure 3-3 on page 64. Note the instances of repeated operations. There are, for example, six carton formers on Line 20. Certainly, this is an area where Heileman may be able to consolidate. We also wondered why there are packing machines and manual packers mixed together in the next operation. This operation seems ripe for a reconfiguration in which the automatic packers can do all the work. There are also a number of different kinds of machines that do essentially the same operation. The questions we will pose for Heileman is whether their product size can be standardized in some way so that only one type of machine is necessary. In short, you can see that a process flow map reveals a lot of opportunities for improvement.

# Statistical Process Control as a Means for Continuous Improvement in Manufacturing

Statistical Process Control (SPC) is an effective method of evaluating a process to identify both desirable and undesirable changes. Armand V. Feigenbaum's book, *Total Quality Control*, contains an excellent discussion of statistical methods. The result of Statistical Process Control is to produce a product which conforms to requirements while the product is in process.

When we teach clients about Statistical Process Control, we have always emphasized that it is more than keeping charts to monitor control of a process. We have looked upon SPC as a way of identifying and eliminating faults within the process with the ultimate aim of shortening cycle time. The flow chart in Figure 3-4 on page 65 shows how to use SPC in this manner. It is important that companies not prepare control charts until they have completed the first six steps. We have seen far too many companies start with control charts and have no results to show for their premature efforts.

# Reengineering through Cycle Time Management

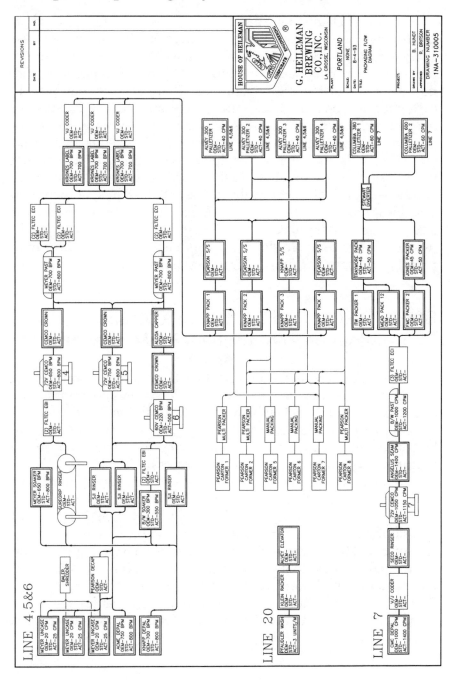

Figure 3-3.

64

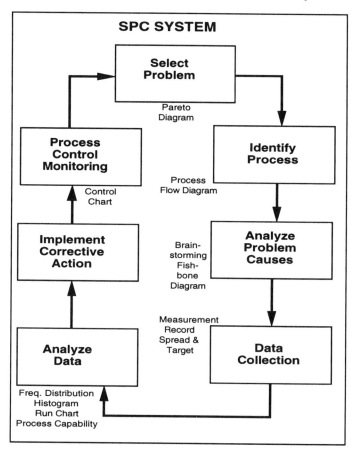

**Figure 3-4.**

We can no longer conduct business in an environment which accepts previous high levels of nonvalue-added activities, scrap, rework, waste and delays. Establishing process control with Cycle Time Management is the new level of excellence and perfection we seek.

## Using Kanban to Reduce Inventory and Maintain a Line of Balance

When improvement teams at our clients decide to balance the production line and supply it only with the material needed to build

## Reengineering through Cycle Time Management

products on order, they often use a Kanban system. Peter Grieco refers to Kanban in his book, *Made in America: The Total Business Concept* (PT Publications, West Palm Beach, FL), as a means to signal a need to the organization. That need communicates the necessity for one of the following activities: produce, replenish, plan or eliminate.

American companies typically employ a Kanban card to signal a demand for pulling material through various internal operations and to signal a demand for replenishing material from other departments or external suppliers. A pull system starts with demand from customers. Sales then signals finished goods with a Kanban card to release the product so that it can be shipped to satisfy the customer's demand. This sets the stage for the issuing of other Kanban cards that

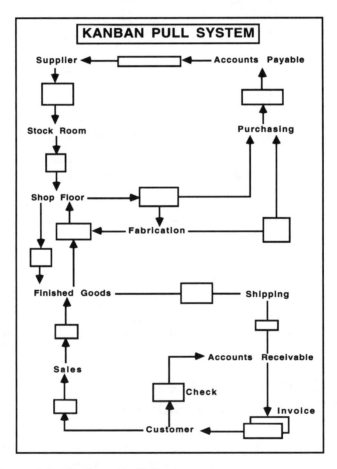

**Figure 3-5. Kanban Pull System.**

signal the process to produce. This combination of signal followed by replenishment continues throughout all of the operations and eventually to the company's suppliers who then replenish the consumed parts, services or raw material. Figure 3-5 shows a typical Kanban pull system.

Kanban systems are an excellent way to cut administrative time. If implemented and used properly, Kanban can eliminate numerous paper and manual transactions. At one client, we were able to help them eliminate the following activities and forms. This action had a very positive effect on cycle time.

### CYCLE TIME IMPROVEMENTS
### <u>MADE POSSIBLE BY KANBAN</u>

- **No requisitions**
- **No purchase order**
- **No receiving ticket**
- **No stocking ticket**
- **No invoicing**

- **No order entry**
- **No packing slip**
- **No receipt transaction**
- **No inventory update**
- **Reduced fax transmissions**

At another client, J.I. Case, we helped implement a Kanban system for eight part numbers at only one location on their plant floor. Three months after the implementation, the savings were recorded as $69,000! Management quickly saw that Kanban was an integral part of Cycle Time Management and began to expand the process.

# Set-Up Reduction's Role
# in Cycle Time Management

Set-up reduction and quick die changes are mandatory in a technology-hungry market. You must encourage your organization to start the process of reducing set-ups both internally on the equipment and externally through the procurement of capital equipment requiring shorter set-up times. These actions are needed in order to remain competitive. Set-up reduction programs have played a significant role in assisting companies to reduce not only the time to set up equipment and processes, but lot sizes and costs as well. In fact, each company must insist that improvement teams pursue more than just time savings. The perception that set-up reduction programs are implemented so that companies will have more time to produce product is only partially true. The real benefits come from cutting lot sizes to one, which allows for more flexibility in meeting customer demands for smaller quantities, lowering inventory and reducing total cycle times. The agile manufacturing we discussed in previous chapters places an emphasis on this high standard of performance. In our book, *Set-Up Reduction: Saving Dollars with Common Sense* (PT Publications, West Palm Beach, FL), we demonstrate that zero set-ups and readily available equipment are vital in attaining an agile manufacturing environment. The benefits of successfully reaching this level are too numerous to mention here.

Set-up reduction will also enable each of you to improve quality and keep up with your competition. The future belongs to those companies which have speed and flexibility. Set-up reduction is not just about replacing nuts and bolts with a quick disconnect apparatus. The technical details are certainly part of set-up reduction, but you cannot expect equipment and tooling changes alone to have as great an impact. Set-up reduction must at least include lot sizing, Zero Inventory (ZI), Just-In-Time (JIT), Total Quality Management (TQM) and Preventive Maintenance (PM) to achieve World Class standards. To be on the leading edge of set-up reduction means that a company will need to integrate it with other cycle time reduction activities in the manufacturing area.

An example of what we are talking about was developed by Tom Petroski and a team at Neodata who reconfigured the process flow in one part of the plant. As the diagram in Figure 3-6 demonstrates, Tom and the Neodata team began by building an opening in the wall ( see #1) between the warehouse and the print shop so that only enough kitted materials needed to complete the job order would be directly delivered. They then installed a roller conveyor from the print shop to bursting (see #2). Inside the print shop, the team devised a scan test which ensured that bar codes were readable and thus reduced scrap as well as labor, material and time.

The team decided to position the bursting machines parallel to each other so that it was necessary for only one operator to run two machines (see #3).

Once forms are bursted, those that need folding are now directed to the folding machine, while those that do not are routed directly to the insert machines (see #4). As for the insert machines, they were positioned back to back so that only five operators were

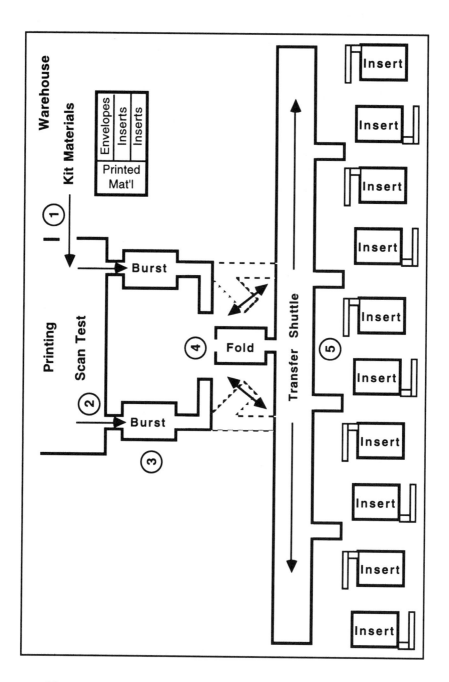

Figure 3-6.

needed to run 10 machines (see #5). The operators are also now responsible for keeping the insert machines up and running. One roving operator loads all the machines and one set-up/mechanic/handler is responsible for material movement.

The team decided to use mailing boxes for the kitted materials. They devised a method to pre-stage all necessary print materials such as envelopes and inserts up front. By weighing out materials, they were assured that they would only use the required quantities of necessary materials. These changes improved handling and ensured that jobs were queued correctly.

The passage opened up in the wall between the warehouse and the print shop eliminated the need of hand-trucking and thus reduced material handling, eliminated staging and reduced the number of units in queue. The focus could then be put on daily printing only of required jobs.

The scan test before production was instrumental in improving quality by preventing bad printing from continuing through the process. This improved the efficiency of material, machines and labor and reduced costs.

As for the process flow, it was low cost to implement and now represented a continual flow instead of a functional process. It improved labor utilization and reduced the head count from 12 to eight. In addition, the changes increased capacity and improved the floor plan. The new methods also helped to develop ownership as operators became cross-trained.

# Total Productive Maintenance: Achieving the Goal of Zero Breakdowns

Total Productive Maintenance (TPM) or zero breakdown maintenance ensures that any equipment used in the manufacturing of a product will be in full operating condition each and every time it needs to be used. The responsibility of a preventive maintenance team is to uncover and solve problems before they interfere with production and contribute to lengthy cycle times. Its goal is to be proactive, instead of reactive, to approach a level where all problems can be predicted and prevented. Its motto is not to fix equipment when it is broken, but to address maintenance issues on a continuous basis so that the equipment is kept in peak running condition. You can begin this process by identifying where problems have occurred in the past and by preparing a Pareto chart after collecting data.

There are a number of excellent computerized systems available to manage and track maintenance, but they are worthless if nobody analyzes the recorded data and then uses it to take corrective action. Unfortunately, many companies collect information about maintenance but use very little of the data to improve the process.

We have found, however, that companies can achieve the following results by employing preventive maintenance programs.

- **Increased machine availability**
- **Reduced spare parts inventory**
- **Improved execution of maintenance work orders**
- **More efficient planning for turnarounds and shutdowns**
- **Faster response to emergency work**
- **Higher return on investments**
- **Smoother maintenance scheduling**
- **Lower total cost**
- **Improved uptime**
- **Increased equipment life**
- **Improved quality**
- **Increased productivity**
- **Improved inventory turns**
- **Improved ability to plan and predict failures based on statistics**
- **Lower cost of quality**
- **Lower purchase cost for MRO items**
- **Shorter cycle times**

Companies must make preventive maintenance a top priority. Otherwise, you will spend a majority of your time putting out fires caused by equipment problems, instead of finding ways to prevent the problems from occurring. Preventive maintenance is vital to the management of cycle time. The key is not to reduce the number of maintenance people. Train these people to do what needs to be done before an equipment breakdown occurs.

## Linking Inventory Management and Cycle Time Management

Out-of-control inventories have been likened to a noose around

71

productivity. Better than 50 percent of a company's assets are tied up in inventory. In a service company, better than 50 percent of the effort expended can be viewed as nonvalue-added and out-of-control. This nonproductive capital is one of the strongest drains on the vitality of American industry. The intent of cycle time reduction is to get the right material to the right place at the right time so that every procedure and operation adds value to the product. The goal of cycle time reduction is to produce or provide in one day all the products or services you need in order to fill customer orders. This will result in less material in the plant since inventory will not sit in storage or queues, adding carrying costs to your bottom line. Figure 3-7 shows these relationships.

Companies make the mistake of looking at inventory purely as an asset. Technically, it is, but it costs money to carry this asset. Inventory carrying costs include such items as:

- **Storage space costs.**
- **Handling equipment costs for stores.**
- **Inventory risk costs.**
- **Inventory service costs.**
- **Capital costs (cost of borrowing money).**

Carrying costs can account for as much as 30 percent of the total value of the inventory. For a more detailed discussion of the cost of inventory, see Chapter 3 of *Activity Based Costing: The Key to World Class Performance* (PT Publications, Inc., West Palm Beach, FL). Cycle time reduction can significantly lower the cost of inventory by reducing the amount of inventory a company will need to satisfy customer requirements.

It is imperative that we begin exploring alternative methods of inventory management, such as those coming under the umbrella of Cycle Time Management. Such inventory management will have the following advantages and benefits:

1. **Improve your competitive position both domestically and internationally.**

2. **Eliminate waste (Inventory, Carrying Costs, Physical Space, Material Handling, etc.).**

3. **Expose unproductive manufacturing processes.**

4. **Minimize obsolescence.**

5. **Introduce flexible manufacturing.**

6. **Respond more quickly to change.**

7. **Meet customer demands quickly.**

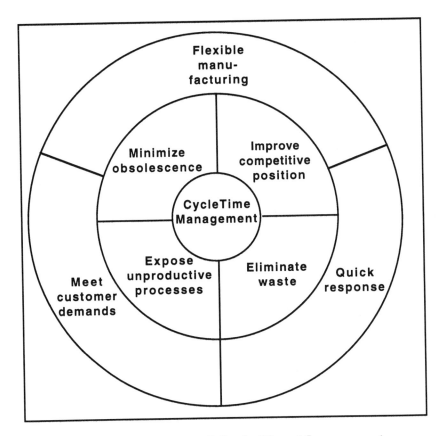

Figure 3-7. Inventory and Cycle Time Management

Safety stocks only solve one problem at the expense of covering up far more serious problems. We think that we can never have a high enough level of inventory, but eliminating high levels of inventory has the important function of exposing hidden problems. Actually dealing with the real problems and not hiding behind walls of inventory allows us to be more flexible/productive in our factories.

## The Relevance of Just-In-Time and Total Quality Control

We have always considered Just-In-Time and Total Quality Control to be more than programs to reduce inventory or to increase quality levels. We have linked the two together into a whole that is greater than its parts and have put the emphasis on JIT/TQC as a way of doing business. In short, we anticipated Cycle Time Management a long time ago. CTM can be seen as JIT/TQC at full maturity. The manufacturing systems of the future will simply not be able to function if defect rates can't come close to achieving Six Sigma levels and if delivery isn't made on time directly to the production line 100 percent of the time. Even Total Quality Management, as practiced, falls somewhat short of the desired goal since it concentrates on the manufacturing and quality assurance areas of an organization. Quality must move beyond these domains to include every facet of a company. Thus, JIT/TQC helps to link manufacturing to the cycle time reduction effort of the whole company.

The most current thought on quality also moves it beyond the company itself and its suppliers to include the voice of the customer as well. The method for translating customer requirements into technical requirements for each stage in the product/process development cycle goes by the name of Quality Function Deployment (QFD). Its goal is to ensure that the objectives and priorities of the company and customers remain focused and that manufacturing control points are identified and maintained.

## Robotics and Automation

Many companies have used the strategy of automating without first reducing cycle time and lot sizes. Such a strategy only nets a small improvement in run time and an insignificant reduction in total cycle time. When using this strategy, we advocate following the Law of Judicious Utilization.

## LAW OF JUDICIOUS UTILIZATION

**Simple solutions are the best use of resources.
Only automate on a cost/benefit basis after other
alternatives have been exhausted.**

With this law in mind, you would eliminate waste and then go out into your company and look at the following areas in which "judicious" automation can be effected.

- **Process**
- **Equipment**
- **Handling**
- **Storage**

- **People**
- **Queue**
- **Move**
- **Wait**

Automation also applies to information technology. Bar coding technology and EDI (Electronic Data Interchange) speed up the flow of information in a company by reducing the number of errors and the unnecessary set-up of data collection. Companies often use bar coding to assist in communicating the status of the flow and in enhancing the reliability of data collection.

Whatever the form of automation or robotics, we support its use. Automation assuredly has its place in a company's future. We're just advising you to use caution, not to fall into the "me too" trap. Use or buy automation only if you have a need for it, not because you heard about some other company who used or bought it. We recommend that you pay for automation out of the savings generated as a result of cycle time reduction, lot size reduction and inventory reduction. This process forces the company to eliminate waste and then automate.

## The New Information Technologies

In order to ensure that manufacturing proceeds concurrently instead of sequentially, it is necessary to have total integration of the information systems in your company. This means the electronic transfer of information within the company, between the company and its suppliers, and between the company and its customers. We have hinted at some examples of this integration before when we discussed custom ordering at the bicycle manufacturer in Japan, customer integrated manufacturing at the Ross Operating Valve Co. in Troy, Michigan and production scheduling at the Saturn plant in Spring Hill, Tenn. But much of this technology is still maturing and is not in widespread use. The opportunity is here, as Vice President Al Gore has noted, to create an information superhighway for the future.

From the perspective of Cycle Time Management in the manufacturing arena, this is what we would like to see in these new information technologies.

- **Strict, universal data exchange standards which would be supported by broadband communication channels.**

- **Ability to share information with all production partners so that collaborative problem solving can be utilized.**

- **Networks which would be able to link all operating areas together on a real-time basis.**

- **User-friendly access to national and international databases of technology.**

- **Electronic transfer of information and data to internal and external customers through integrated databases and electronic data capture devices.**

- **Networked simulation and modeling applications which can be used to evaluate product and process design concurrently.**

There are a number of people who are trying to turn this wish list into reality. Factory America Net (FAN) is envisioned as a network which would allow companies of all sizes to bid electronically on requests for proposals, to engage in concurrent engineering projects among several companies, to search databases for compatible suppliers or partners and to find out who is looking for the products they build or services they provide. How would connecting to this network cut cycle time? First, it could help you from reinventing the wheel. Second, it could help you find best-in-class practices to emulate. Third, it could steer you toward creative partnerships in which each company performs the set of actions which it does best. The overall effect of integrated information networks would be to shrink the current number of layers or departments through which information is channeled. The more information you can bring to a problem, the better your chances of reducing cycle time.

# How to Perform a Cost/Benefit Analysis of Manufacturing Technologies

Unfortunately, many efforts to introduce technology enhancements within an organization meet with little or no support. This isn't necessarily because management is resistant to change, but because the introducers have failed to provide alternatives and convince management that the change will benefit the organization's performance. From our experience, that means you need to figure out the return on investment. The key to gaining management commitment is to answer the question of how does it affect the bottom line. Cycle time savings must be defined in terms of dollars. A cost vs. benefit analysis of technology improvements should include the following:

- **Solid evidence of opportunities for improvement.**

- **Strategy for long-term/short-term improvements.**

- **How much it will cost to correct issues.**

- **Profile of potential savings.**

Cost accountants can assist improvement teams in the preparation of such analyses, as is demonstrated in *Activity Based Costing: The Key to World Class Performance* (PT Publications, West Palm Beach, FL). They can help determine what the savings will be when a new technology is implemented in an organization. This means that the people in a company must first be trained to understand new technologies and how costs will be affected by their implementations.

# Reengineering through Cycle Time Management

# Some Solutions to Problems in Manufacturing Technology

We have addressed a number of new manufacturing technologies in this chapter and we have looked at how they can be used to reduce cycle time. How would these ideas and action plans be applied to the problems at the Blackbox Company? As you may remember, we noticed large piles of inventory around the factory floor, no evidence of any statistical charts, long cycle times and no structured maintenance program. The solution to these problems is to initiate several work teams to begin education and training in Just-In-Time, Statistical Process Control, Cycle Time Reduction and Preventive Maintenance.

The Blackbox Company is ready to attack the year 2000 and move up the evolutionary ladder in order to become a World Class agile manufacturer. We see our job as helping to pave the way. There are two initial steps to take on this journey and both entail breaking down barriers. The first barrier to tear down is the wall between the Blackbox Company and its suppliers. This wall makes each side into an adversary, instead of a Supply Management partner. In the next chapter, we will discuss this area in great detail.

The second barrier is the wall built around each department or function within the company itself. The adoption of new manufacturing technologies will require companies like Blackbox to adopt a new paradigm of operation as well. Consequently, we spent much of our time going over the paradigm shift outlined earlier in this chapter. We showed all levels in the organization that a more open system based on concurrency would benefit all and would make Blackbox the type of company which would survive and prosper well into the next century. In Chapter Seven, we will introduce you to the techniques required to achieve major changes in your company.

# Summary

### The Paradigm Shift
Each function of a company cannot be viewed as an island unto itself in the company's organization. It must interface with customer- and supplier-related activities in an effort to reduce

cycle time. Cycle Time Management in each functional arena is about shifting from the lean style exemplified by Just-In-Time and Total Quality Control to a flexible style exemplified by the philosophy of an agile company.

### Group Technology
The analysis of operations and activities to determine which are value-added and which are nonvalue-added. Analysis is followed by the reconfiguration of the process flow to eliminate waste in movement, inventory and set-ups.

### Statistical Process Control (SPC)
SPC is a way of identifying and eliminating faults within the process with the ultimate aim of preventing defects. Processes are monitored using statistical techniques which reveal when a process needs adjustment to stay within upper and lower control limits.

### Kanban
Kanban is typically used to signal a demand for pulling material through a process and as a signal to other departments or outside suppliers to replenish material. Kanban systems are an excellent way of cutting administrative time.

### Changeovers
The aim of Changeover Reduction is not only to cut set-up times, but to reduce lot sizes and increase flexibility. The ideal changeover time is zero; the ideal lot size is one.

### Zero Breakdown
The responsibility of a preventive maintenance team is to uncover and solve problems before they interfere with production and contribute to lengthy cycle times. Total Productive Maintenance ensures that any equipment used in manufacturing a product will be in full operating condition, capable of producing quality product at full operating speed all the time.

### Inventory Management
The intent of cycle time reduction is to get the right material to the right place at the right time in the right quantity. Safety stocks solve one problem at the expense of covering up far more serious problems.

## Reengineering through Cycle Time Management

### Just-In-Time (JIT) and Total Quality Control (TQC)

Both are more than programs to reduce inventory and to increase quality levels. We have viewed JIT and TQC as a way of doing business which leads to Cycle Time Management.

### Robotics and Automation

We are in favor of both robotics and automation. Much of the agile company will not be possible without them, but we define both terms much more broadly than many other people. Any simple solution that eliminates waste is automation.

### Information Technology

The new information technologies are essential to the operation of an organization based on the concurrency and agile models. Information must move freely and instantaneously to support quick and precise decision making.

## Action Steps

1) Form a team to benchmark, map processes, develop strategies, identify manufacturing technologies and report their findings to management.

2) Identify the problem areas within each functional area. Refer to the suggestions given throughout this chapter. Each of these areas represents an opportunity to reduce cycle time.

3) Encourage the discussion and adoption of a strategic plan for introducing new service and manufacturing technologies within your organization.

4) Select a pilot area from the list you developed in Step 2.

5) Perform a cost/benefit analysis of the various proposals for addressing the issues in the pilot area.

6) Formulate and implement an action plan for introducing a new service and manufacturing technology into the pilot area.

# Chapter Four: Supply Base Management

When we turn back to the relationship map (page 26) to take a look in terms of Supply Management, an opportunity for improvement seems to jump off the page. The Purchasing and Production Planning departments operate almost independent of each other, a condition we see in companies everywhere. The only time the two departments at the company communicated was when Planning alerted Purchasing of its material needs. And that was typically late. This is a state of affairs that simply cannot exist in the modern corporation. We also knew from our assessment that there was no buyer/planner function. And, to make matters worse, buyers' performances were measured by Purchase Price Variance (PPV), a measurement to determine how much current purchases deviate from standard prices. Thus, there was little time allotted to work on cycle time reduction and process mapping.

## Power Purchasing

After identification of problems, the most important step in Total Cycle Time Management is the process mapping of the purchasing system as it is today in order to locate all of the "white spaces" in the system. The next step would be to map the supplier process or the total acquisition cycle. Then, as each function reviews its piece of the overall cycle time, they can work at the detail level in the effort to achieve an overall reduction. The purpose of mapping the purchasing system is to coordinate all efforts made by a company's design, quality assurance, marketing, manufacturing, procurement

# Reengineering through Cycle Time Management

and finance functions along with the supplier as they seek to reduce time to market. Mapping is a process which makes extensive use of Purchasing's involvement in the satisfaction of customers.

It is equally important for management to recognize Purchasing's contribution to profitability. In order to reap the benefits of process mapping, a company must establish a proactive training and education program as well as a cross-functional team to address the issues brought forth by the process map. Performance is then measured not only in terms of Purchasing involvement in process mapping, but on their use of Cycle Time Management to reduce cycle time and eliminate waste in all nonvalue-added areas.

As you can see, there has been a paradigm shift in the field of purchasing. The flow chart in Figure 4-1 show how one of our clients, the engineering services giant ABB (Asea Brown Boverii) Semi-Conductor operation has reengineered its purchasing function to eliminate all the steps in the process that do not need to be executed. We also would like to point out that process mapping helps to identify related interfaces which might be affected. Our software, Process Vision, which was developed by Antares, provides you with a tool to perform process mapping at all levels. It also allows you to analyze the process steps for duplication of data points and shows you how one task links to another.

The first time that this process was mapped by a team, there were about 25 flow points. After the team reviewed that draft, they added many more points which were missed in the first pass. The purchasing function depicted in Figure 4-1 is an improvement over their previous process attempts. But, they still continue today to reengineer this function. The purchasing cycle shown here basically has a requisition cycle with subcycles in which import licenses are obtained, purchase orders are registered in their computer system, a "poison stamp" for hazardous chemicals is obtained and a cost test (dollar value) is applied to see whether authorization for the purchase order is required by the president. The purchase order then goes to the supplier and, at the same time, a copy is sent to Finance to initiate the payment cycle to the supplier when the product and invoice is received. There is an acknowledgment cycle after the supplier receives the purchase order. The next major component begins with the arrival of goods at the factory. This initiates an inspection and test cycle. Good material is put into stock and bad material initiates another cycle in which the supplier is notified.

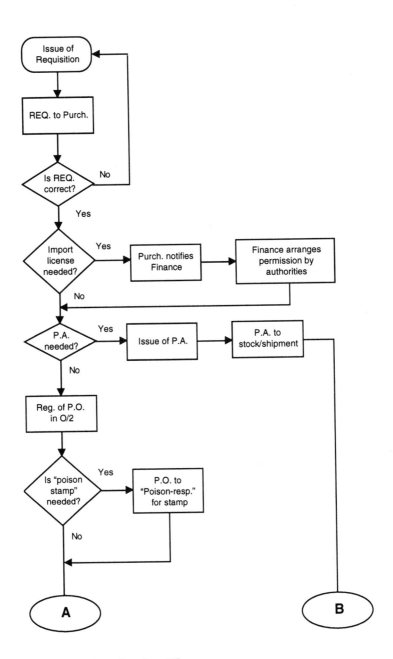

**Figure 4-1a. Purchasing Flow**

# Reengineering through Cycle Time Management

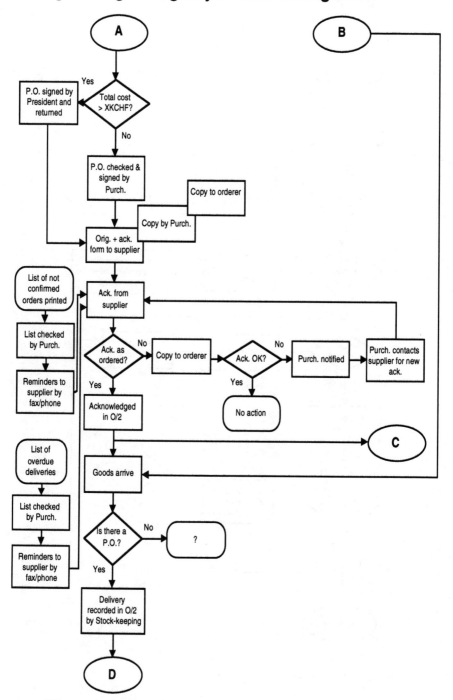

Figure 4-1b. Purchasing Flow

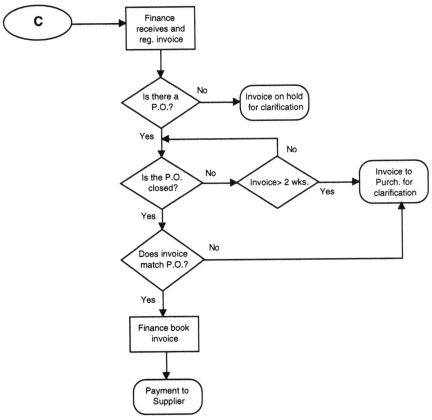

**Figure 4-1c. Purchasing Flow**

Even though this is a snapshot of the purchasing cycle, that does not mean that there is no room for continuing to cut cycle time even further after each review. For example, in the requisition component, we see an immediate need for the introduction of Electronic Data Interchange (EDI) and Bar Coding applications. This would eliminate checking requisitions to see if they are accurate and EDI would obviously eliminate the step requiring somebody to enter the requisition into the company's computer system, since it is already put in the system by the receiving function. A "poison stamp" could be put on by the supplier and would be updated automatically from a database at the company. A similar operation could be set up for the president's cost test, but we would want to ask a few questions before we implemented that subsystem. We would

# Reengineering through Cycle Time Management

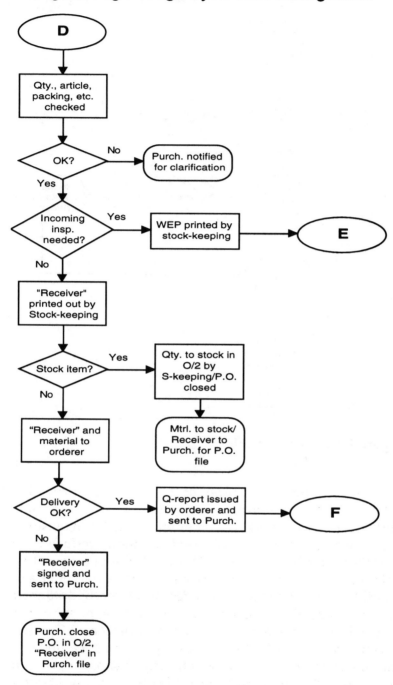

**Figure 4-1d. Purchasing Flow**

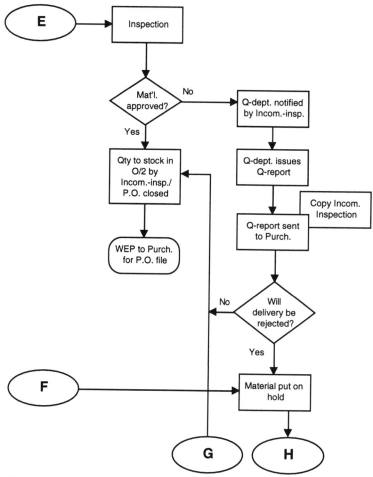

**Figure 4-1e. Purchasing Flow**

want to know why the president needs to sign off on purchase orders and would instruct a team to brainstorm the present way of doing this. We are sure in the age of delegating responsibility to the lowest level that the company could at least begin by limiting the number of times this subcycle is invoked. Lastly, there would be no need to check purchase orders or send copies to other departments with EDI. This would all be done automatically by the system.

EDI would also greatly improve the next major component of the purchasing cycle which involves sending the purchase order to the supplier. The company could probably eliminate the entire

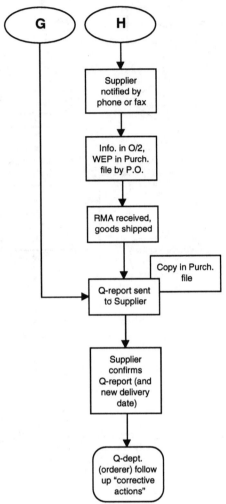

**Figure 4-1f. Purchasing Flow**

acknowledgments subcycle as well as the production of copies and the placement of acknowledgments in the company's computer system. EDI would also eliminate the necessity of sending paper invoices to Finance since that department would receive the information via internal EDI.

Once the goods arrive from the supplier, the implementation of a bar coding system would greatly cut cycle time by eliminating the need to check for purchase orders. As for inspection, our first question is "why?" If these were certified suppliers, why would you need to have an inspection cycle at all? The same goes for the placement of good material into stock. Why isn't it delivered directly to the point of need? And finally, why is there bad material? There shouldn't be if suppliers are certified. Our first piece of advice in cutting cycle time in this area would be to implement a supplier certification process to eliminate these cycles completely.

## Early Supplier Involvement

We need to introduce, with R&D, a step in the mapping process which looks at reducing the development cycle for new products and processes. With the use of ESI (Early Supplier Involvement), we have an opportunity to use suppliers in cost reduction and component development. These suppliers are partners in helping us design products which use fewer components, allow quicker response, cost less to manufacture and exhibit World Class quality. Costs will go down and profits will increase in this type of arrangement. In addition, the supplier is given a long-term contract which often guarantees business for the life of the product, given that the supplier meets requirements. Process mapping must allow for purchasing to work with suppliers in shortening lead times, eliminating paper-work and lowering costs.

## The True Meaning of Supplier Partnerships

Supplier partnerships are the most effective way of bringing total cost down, increasing an organization's flexibility, learning new technologies, and benchmarking World Class practices in order to achieve Six Sigma quality and dramatically improve developmental and operational speed. This demands a breed of supplier who not only can produce the part we need, but one that can help us design it and integrate the processes necessary to assemble the finished product. The influence of the customer company will need to extend beyond the level of suppliers to subsuppliers two to four levels down. We must map the external supply chain process. The emphasis, throughout the supply chain, will be on shrinking cycle time and lead times. Such a partnership can be accomplished by providing assistance to suppliers in cycle time reduction, technology, quality and cost improvements as intensive supplier training.

## Reengineering through Cycle Time Management

The goal of supplier partnerships is to help your suppliers achieve cycle time reductions and for them to reduce lead times to your plant.

# Managing External Cycle Time

Commodity management is a Supply Management technique in which a team engages in activities which meet the overall supply strategy of the company. These teams are involved in efforts to reduce the supply base, consolidate pricing, reduce cost, guarantee quality levels and delivery schedules, and reduce cycle time. It is their responsibility as well to oversee the selection, qualification and certification of suppliers as outlined in several other books in PT Publications' professional series. (See page 167 for a complete listing of its purchasing books.) Quality levels are attained through quality surveys, measurements, process improvements, and training and education programs initiated by a team working with external suppliers. Pro-Tech has been providing educational services in these areas for a number of years to external suppliers and customers to aid them in their development.

The underlying philosophy of management of the external supply base is continuous improvement. Those suppliers who achieve the goal of consistent annual improvement should be recognized for their achievement. Goals need to be measured to determine year-to-year improvement in cycle time reduction. You should expect your suppliers to improve their performance each year.

This is what occurred at one of our clients, a cosmetic company engaged in a cycle time reduction program. The company had a printer who was printing the outside packaging for their bottled products. When we arrived, the printer had already agreed to delivery of smaller lot sizes, but they were still running large lot sizes since there was a great deal of make-ready, or set-up, time in the printing process. In fact, they were warehousing the large lots of packaging and shipping small lots to the cosmetic company as needed. This obviously kept the printer's costs higher and prohibited them from being flexible enough to respond to changes in packaging design or size.

The cosmetic company approached the printer and told them that they appreciated the frequent delivery, but that what they now wanted was to link the printer's production to their production requirements. "We want you to produce and ship in the quantities we demand," the cosmetic company informed the printer, "not to just ship in those quantities."

At this point, we began working with the printer to find ways to satisfy the requirements of the cosmetic firm, a very important customer of the printer. We focused first on set-up reduction and the result was a better than 50% reduction in make-ready time. There were two ways in which the printer was able to achieve this significant cycle time reduction using methods detailed in *Set-Up Reduction: Saving Dollars with Common Sense* (PT Publications, Inc., West Palm Beach, FL). First, they adopted the use of standard register blocks to align the printing. This virtually eliminated the adjustment period of the old registering method. Second, they cleaned ink rollers externally, using another set of rollers on the press while the first set was being cleaned.

Another way the cosmetic company was able to reduce cycle time was to begin the practice of the buying of capacity. This is how that practice works. Let's say the lead time from the printer is four weeks. Of course, it doesn't actually take four weeks to print the product. The lengthy lead time is a function of the printer's backlog, not of its process. By analyzing the lead time and identifying backlog as the significant factor, the cosmetic company decided to buy capacity (that is, they bought scheduled times for printing in advance), instead of the printed product. When the cosmetic company's scheduled printing time arrived, the printer would call and find out what products they wanted printed and then set up the press accordingly. Thus, the cosmetic company was able to get their printed product, but did not have to commit to the specific product until the shortest possible lead time. An ingenious solution!

# Summary

### What is Supply Cycle Time Management?
Supply Cycle Time Management can be defined as the uninterrupted flow of 100% acceptable materials delivered on time, 100% of the time, at optimal cost from suppliers and which meet customer requirements. In the Supply Base Management cycle, a company gathers facts about a supplier, designs quality improvement processes, puts them into practice, and then audits and maintains the process based on the results which it is gathering and interpreting.

### Reengineering through Cycle Time Management

**Process Mapping of Purchasing Activities**

The process by which a team maps a purchasing system in order to locate all of the "white spaces" in the system. Each function then reviews its piece of the overall cycle time at the detail level in the effort to achieve an overall reduction. Requires the coordination of efforts made by a company's design, quality assurance, marketing, manufacturing, procurement and finance functions along with the supplier as they seek to reduce time to market.

**Supply Base Management Benchmarking Performance Measurements**

Reducing the cycle time of Supply Management requires gathering and analyzing performance data from your suppliers. Data must then be used to benchmark your company against the best and develop actions which continuously improve the process or product.

## Action Steps

1) Conduct a process mapping of your purchasing cycle to determine where you can reduce cycle time.

2) Engage your suppliers in an ESI effort to reduce the development cycle and to seek ways to reduce the lead times of new product introduction.

3) Work with suppliers to reduce the lead times of their production and delivery cycle times.

# Chapter Five: Marketing/Sales/ Customer Service Cycle

Most of the problems identified in the Marketing/Sales/Customer Service cycle at the Blackbox Co. can be attributed to a lack of coordinated teamwork. This particular cycle is one that crosses a number of departmental boundaries in a company today. That is undoubtedly why we often see what is a critical part of any business as blocks of fragmented operations with no real connections between them. At the Balckbox Co., for example, the Customer Service functions consisting of customer consulting, training and troubleshooting have no direct contact with Marketing or Sales. In fact, the only connection is through the customers which means that Sales generally hears about issues and opportunities in Consulting Services and Customer Training from customers. Marketing is even one more step removed. They hear about what the company is doing in the area of customer service from Sales who get the information, as we have pointed out, from customers. (See Figure 1-3 on page 26 for a diagram of these relationships.)

The unnecessary tangle of communications resembles a game we used to play as children. In "Gossip," one child would write down a story and then whisper it to the child next to him. She would then whisper it to the child next to her and so on around the room until the last child told the final version of the story out loud. Then, the first child would read aloud the story he had written down. I can remember laughing with all my friends when we heard how different the two stories were. It's not a laughing matter, however, when companies do the same thing. The Blackbox Co. is in danger if it cannot get departments within the cycle to communicate the "original story" to each other.

## Reengineering through Cycle Time Management

We also noticed that the fragmentation was even more serious than the lack of communication. The company performs the very commendable function of sending out training teams to customers to help them maximize the use of products. This program has built up a tremendous amount of goodwill for the company and is one of the major reasons why it has a stellar reputation as a company that cares. Incredibly, however, the fruits of this effort are mostly squandered with the absence of Marketing's involvement on these teams. We saw this serious flaw in the Marketing/Sales/Customer Service cycle as a sorely missed opportunity. The feedback that Marketing could gather on these training visits would be of untold value. Marketing could use the gathered information to help Engineering design even better product models and to aid Sales in generating and closing deals.

One last observation we made was in the area of support cycle time which Marketing provides to Sales in the form of brochures and manuals. We found that 75% of this material was out-of-date and customers' complaints were increasing at an alarming rate.

They must begin to think of their customers as an integral part of their business. In doing so, they could drastically reduce the Marketing/Sales/Customer Service cycle. Key issues about direction and a course of action are covered in this chapter.

# Marketing/Sales/Customer Service Cycle Time

It is critically important to map the customer ordering process throughout the cycle in order to identify all the activities and their times. Figure 5-1 illustrates the first step in identifying the relationships and "white spaces" in the cycle. The diagram demonstrates the typical sequence of major phases in the cycle and their duration.

Our task is to take each of these phases and map each step and activity within the existing process with as much detail as possible. The purpose of this is to use the map (an example is shown in Figure 5-2) to evaluate the process in order to eliminate all nonvalue-added activities. For example, Sales Activity, which is shown as taking 40 days in Figure 5-1, breaks down into the activities shown in Figure 5-2. The next step is to determine how long each of these activities take and which ones can be reduced. The goal to keep in mind is that the best way to reduce cycle time is to eliminate the activity. If the activity cannot be eliminated, it should be consolidated with another activ-

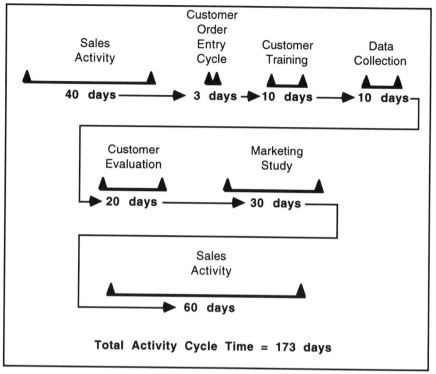

**Figure 5-1.**

ity. If it cannot be eliminated or conslidated, then it should be minimized. Most companies will spend a significant amount of time trying to automate or computerize the activities in Figure 5-2 in their efforts to reduce cycle time. Our recommendation is that you first look for low-cost or no-cost solutions. They are there if you are serious about using teams to identify opportunities for progressive change. Teams, of course, will not only identify the challenge but show ways to reduce or eliminate the cycle time delay. Your teams will be aided in their evaluations by utilizing the assessment questions we have included later in this chapter.

## Early Customer Involvement

The Marketing/Sales/Customer Service cycle is undergoing a radical transformation in the last decade of this century. The changes will be with us far into the next century. The principal development has been a move to involve the customer earlier in the process of

# Reengineering through Cycle Time Management

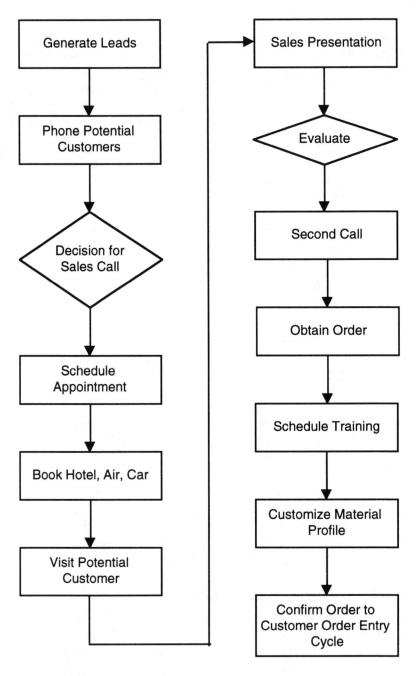

Figure 5-2.

manufacturing a product or providing a service. This development can be seen as a mirror image of the development of strategic partnerships with suppliers. Some organizations, from automakers to health care providers, have even coined a new term to call their customers — prosumers. A prosumer is a customer who is actively involved in the production or provision of a product or service which meets expectations. We have already given the example of the Saturn automobile in which prosumers select the features they want on their cars and these demands are forwarded by computer directly to the production planning department of the plant.

We also believe that prosumers need to understand the internal capabilities of your company. Together, you can work to achieve these characteristics of the company of the future:

- **Flexibility to develop customized products and services in order to provide profit potential to both companies and to shorten the cycle time.**

- **Development of a distribution network which provides direct shipment from the manufacturer or service provider to the customer's Point of Use/Point of Sale (POS).**

- **Establishment of long-term, internal/external partnerships and strategic business alliances focused on cycle time reductions.**

Efforts are aimed toward gaining profitability for both your company and your customer. Companies will need to act more like service industries. In a talk given by Joel Goldhar of the Illinois Institute of Technology at Motorola University, he emphasized our conclusions.

Even though there will be sweeping changes in this area of your business, this transformation is actually a refinement of a much older concept — meeting customer expectations. In the future, companies will need to be flexible enough to meet customer expectations. If expectations change, then companies need to change to meet customer requirements. The problem with many companies is that they fail to determine what is needed or wanted by their customers. This can be remedied by reducing the cycle time in the Marketing /Sales/ Customer Service cycle. Let's take a look at what areas you will need to address and the questions you will need to ask yourself. This is the

## Reengineering through Cycle Time Management

first step in Cycle Time Management of this important facet of your organization.

# Order Entry

Customer orders must be processed correctly and without delay in order to bring the Marketing /Sales /Customer Service cycle under control. Order entry has an impact on every facet of this cycle. The assessment which follows will help you to identify where your process has weaknesses which contribute to long cycle times. Use it to identify those places and to construct solutions.

1. How many customer orders are received each month?_____

   How many line items on each order (Average)?_____

   How many ship dates on each item (Average)?_____

2. How many open customer orders are there at any one time?

   _____

3. What are typical order-to-ship lead times quoted to customers?

   PRODUCT (LINE)                    LEAD TIME

   _____        _____

   _____        _____

   _____        _____

   _____        _____

4. What is the average lead time required by customers in your industry? _____

5. What percent of orders are shipped by the promised date?
   _____

6. Is the promised date the customer request/required date?
   _____Yes _____No

7. Does manufacturing have input in determining promise date?
   _____Yes _____No

8. What is the average number of days late of all orders?
   _____

9. What is the percentage (on average) of line item fill? ____%

10. How is a customer notified of late shipment?
    _____

11. When is a customer notified of late shipment?
    ___Problem Discovery ___Ship Date ___After Ship Date

12. What type of order changes are experienced between order entry and shipment?

    Additions?_____

    Deletions?_____

    Date Changes?_____

    Quantity Changes?_____

    Specification Changes?_____

    Ship to Changes?_____

    Other_____

13. Who specifies the mode of transportation/carrier?
    _____

14. Is there a certification program for carriers? __Yes __No

15. **What percent of sales do service part orders represent?**_____

16. **What customer service policies does the company have?**

   _____

   _____

   _____

17. **How long does it take to enter an order?** ____Days ____Hours

18. **Are shipments from stock or made to order?** ____Stock ____Made to Order

19. **Is there an application for a Bill of Material configuration type module?**

   _____

   _____

20. **What is the staffing level of this function?**

   _____

21. **How are customer orders promised in relationship to capacity?**

   _____

   _____

You can use the preceding evaluation questions and others in this chapter in two ways. First, before the mapping process in order to guide you in identifying all of the activities and "white spaces" in the process. Second, after the mapping process, to help you identify nonvalue-added activities to reduce or eliminate. Either way, a process map is essential to cycle time reduction. A software product called Process Vision provides a tool to ease this mapping exercise.

Questions, like the ones above, can give you measurements which will serve as baselines for understanding the condition of your company today. The activities shown in Figure 5-2 typically take three days. Your goal would be to reduce this by half and, when you reach that goal, set another goal for another 50 percent reduction. We call this our "Fifty Percent Rule." Keep cutting the cycle time by half until it approaches zero.

## Forecast and Planning

What percentage of the time does your forecast reflect actual sales levels? As actual sales materialize, a discrepancy often develops between what Marketing has forecasted and the actual sales figures. This varying demand causes some products to move ahead of schedule and some to be delayed or cancelled entirely. Consequently, a company finds itself in the middle of an ever more confusing situation in which schedules are not met and where there is significant backlog, work-in-process, raw material and finished inventory. Planning for production, procurement and development schedules depends on short-term, accurate forecasting. The closer forecasts are to actual demand, the closer you are to achieving accurate Cycle Time Management.

One way of bringing this cycle under control is to measure how large or small the error is between the forecast and reality and then map the process. But be careful about using this method too broadly. For example, let's imagine your company measures forecast error by product group and total dollars. At the end of the year, Marketing announces that they have met their objectives and hit the forecast within one percent. But let's look more closely. They had, within that product group, a major item miss of 30% and another overestimate of 31%. What has actually happened is that two large errors have washed each other out. To remedy this situation, we believe that Marketing must measure forecasting error on a finer scale. They should be measuring forecasting error by item, rather than in the aggregate.

Before you begin measuring forecasting error, however, we advise you to answer the following questions. They are designed to

# Reengineering through Cycle Time Management

aid you in identifying cycle time opportunities in your company within the area of forecasting and planning:

1. **How do delivery dates and customer lead times get established?**

   _____

   _____

   _____

2. **Does management review and approve both the sales and production plan?**
   ____Yes ____No

3. **Does the sales forecast get recognition and reconciliation by manufacturing and sales?**
   ____Yes ____No

   **If yes, how?**

   _____

   _____

4. **How does planning get feedback from purchasing and production of any requirements that cannot be met?**

   _____

   _____

   _____

5. **Is the sales function informed of engineering change orders?**
   ____Yes ____No

6. **Is there adequate assessment of change order impact on customer delivery?**
   ____Yes ____No

7. **Do customer orders flow through operations and planning?**

_____

_____

_____

8. **Describe the feedback loop for order dates or quantities that cannot be met:**

_____

_____

_____

9. **Are long-range manufacturing plans cognizant of market plans for new products and engineering introduction of new technologies?**
      ____Yes ____No

   **How?**_____

   _____

   _____

   _____

We leave you with the task of reviewing and process mapping your own forecasting cycle. In fact, you should consider whether it is necessary to have a forecast. You can achieve a huge cycle time reduction by booking orders directly to your internal capability. When Peter L Grieco, Jr. worked for Steve Jobs at Apple Computer, Jobs refused to provide a forecast to the team. He said that the factory must produce product or service customers daily based on what the sales group had sold.

# Customer Satisfaction

All too often, companies accept that customer satisfaction cannot be measured quantitatively. Instead, they rely on their perceptions and "feel-good" guesses, rather than facts. We believe that customer satisfaction can be made into a comparative measure which identifies what we are spending to achieve satisfaction versus the identifiable costs of customers not being satisfied. Let's look at customer delivery cycle time performance as an example of how we can improve customer satisfaction by focusing on its reduction. First, here are the measurements we need to take:

- **What percentage of your customer deliveries are on-time? ___%**

- **How many past due orders are there in terms of dollars ___ and line items ___.**

- **What percentage of on-time delivery does your customer demand? ___%**

Then map and measure your actual shipping date against the date requested by the customer. Again, this measurement should be broken down by customer, service and product in order to detect where problems are occurring. We advocate that you establish a goal of a 100% service level to customer request date. Once established, you measure actual shipping versus the shipping plan on a monthly, quarterly and year-to-date schedule. Remember to include past due orders which should be rolled forward into the current month. Your company's performance should be measured on the sum of past due orders and the current month which will require you to make up the backlog as well as the current month's orders.

It is also vital for your company to measure the total scope of customer satisfaction. While measurements in this area are sometimes imprecise, they are essential in providing a litmus test of performance in the marketplace. Measurements should include:

1. **Percent of repeat sales to existing customer base _____**

2. **Number of complaints against orders shipped _____**

3.  **Warranty claims**

    **Number of occurrences by type/by customer** _____

    **Number of reoccurrences by type/by customer** _____

    **Warranty dollars  $_____**

    **Number of repairs by age category of the product _____**

4.  **Unquantified measurements**

    **Market surveys on performance (quality, delivery, function, etc.)**

    **Internal customer surveys (employee surveys)**

5.  **Are other functional areas, besides customer service, used to survey/contact customers? (e.g., production workers, etc.) ____Yes ____No**

6.  **Are customers included in the design review process/ design for producibility? ____Yes ____No**

7.  **How would you describe your reputation with the majority of your customers?**

    _____

    _____

    _____

The preceding questions will provide you with suggestions as to where you can start to measure cycle time. An example of one such measure would be the time between customer orders. We can use the data obtained from this measurement to provide us with new directions in advertising, sales calls, marketing, service enhancement and many other decision points. All too often, we assume that nothing can be done to improve cycle time in these areas, but we are very wrong if we accept that assumption as true.

## Sales and Marketing

The sales force represents your company to the customer. It is essential that they become a part of your Cycle Time Management process in their day-to-day dealings with the customer base. This requires the coordination of the entire organization of your company.

At the Cyrix Corporation, for example, we put together a proposal for the design and implementation of a Sales Force Automation (SFA) system. Our objective was to design an automation process geared toward the future and which would assist the sales group in implementing marketing strategies, as well as improve communication throughout the organization. We began by interviewing and assessing both the internal and external infrastructures to determine where Cyrix was at present and define where Cyrix needs to be in the future. We utilized the following steps:

1.  Define the objectives of Cyrix and establish design strategies.

2.  Determine which areas need to be addressed and put them in a sequential format.

3.  Define the sales organization's short- and long-term business needs.

4.  Review the research and availability of software relating to the Sales Force Automation project.

5.  Identify the specific system specifications.

6.  Identify both internal and external customer/supplier requirements.

7.  Prepare a system architecture for discussion.

We also needed to detail the process of information flow as it presently existed. Once this was completed, we then worked with the management team to reengineer the process to meet World Class standards.

On the strategic front, we also wanted to integrate the company's database in order to address the following issues in system architecture:

1. Demographic profile of the customer base.

2. Psychographic considerations — publications, product reviews and service offerings.

3. History of actual products purchased and usage of those devices.

4. Data to review size of potential market.

5. Status of buying cycle — needs, evaluations, negotiations, stocking, allocation and usage.

6. Communications process to address opportunities.
   • Commodities of customers.
   • Reports that analyze current requirements.
   • Generation of output necessary to drive sales process.

7. Formatted or ad-hoc reports providing information to sales.

8. Facilitate management of leads to the field.

Our approach included interviewing key sales personnel about how they perform their jobs on a daily basis. The intent was to determine how Cyrix stood in relation to these critical areas:

• Benchmarking World Class standards.

• Responsibility and decision-making of the sales organization.

• Communication through work flow.

• Direct customer communication to Cyrix's MRP II environment.

• Price, cost and budget information and data.

- Customer credit positioning and history.
- Key information about the customer in the database.
- Trends in territory performance.
- Travel and expense reporting.
- Commissions and contract reporting.
- Trends analysis vs. forecasting.
- Credit returns and policies.
- Tracking of customer quotations.
- Cycle time in the sales process.
- Contract relationships for a representatives' network.
- Quick response programs.
- Evaluation, benchmarking and control performance.
- Distribution requirements.
- Literature, advertisement and promotional material.
- Technical specifications and report requirements.
- EDI capability and reporting.

The list above defined key characteristics when assessing sales field requirements. We then utilized the techniques employed at Motorola, Federal Express, L.L. Bean and other major corporations which use automation techniques between the field and their home offices. The general scope of this project was to use some short-term solutions that could then be used to develop the long-term Sales Force Automation system.

## Measurements

Although measurement systems which focus on financial issues directly related to dollars spent or earned are considered accepted and auditable, we feel that, in many cases, they restrict the process of Cycle Time Management. One of the reasons why is that they fail to report and control nonfinancial cost measures. Such measurements can often expose what is causing the cycle time to be wasteful and lengthy. For example, companies look at the labor, material and overhead costs of building a product or providing a service, but they rarely ask themselves what it costs their company for wasteful activities such as the following:

**WHAT DOES IT COST . . .**

- **For a customer to complain?**

- **For materials to sit?**

- **To miss a delivery?**

- **For indirect labor?**

- **To process a sales order?**

- **For 24-hour 800-number coverage?**

- **For customization vs. standardization?**

- **To utilize the customer service function?**

- **For field service repairs?**

- **For material acquisitions?**

These activities are not normally considered when cycle time is addressed, but they must be in the future. However, their existence causes dollars to be spent on numerous wasteful activities. And the costs are usually high and therefore offer the largest opportunities for savings. In one company we worked with, for example, the cost of a customer to complain was analyzed and found to be $850. And this cost did not include the replacement cost of a new product. In doing this analysis, the company also captured the number of complaints which were processed during the month in order to compute the total cost of customer complaints. Here is what they found:

| Number of Complaints | x | Complaint $s | = | Total Cost of Customer Complaints |
|---|---|---|---|---|
| 7 | x | $850 | = | $5,950 |

This was the cost for one month for one product. Think about how much it would cost your company when you have a process out of control. We advise conducting a similar type of analysis. We also recommend that all elements should be logged in categories, using the seven tools of quality. (See Figure 5-3.) Then you can utilize the Pareto graph to identify and work on the largest cost drivers. This method will provide you with the greatest amount of savings in the year that follows. Gone are the days of reducing direct labor to achieve these levels of savings. Now, more can be saved from addressing nonvalue-added activities, materials, resources and indirect activities. The plan outlined above of mapping the process and constructing Pareto charts is the most powerful way to combat waste.

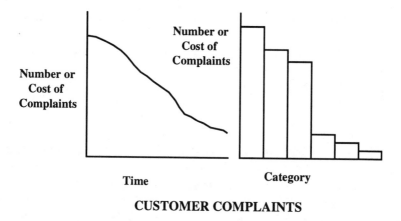

**CUSTOMER COMPLAINTS**

**Figure 5-3.**

# Some Solutions to Problems in the Marketing/Sales/Customer Service Cycle

Our solutions to the problems described at the beginning of this chapter were straightforward. We immediately helped the Company set up a feedback cycle among Customer Service, Marketing, Training, Consulting Services and Sales. Now each department would get first-hand information about what customers want. We also staffed the team with a representative from Marketing to accompany the training group on visits to customer sites. A number of the team members quickly suggested that the company add a representative from Design Engineering and Production to the team as well. We suggested that representatives from Design and Production also accompany the training teams on a part-time, rotating schedule.

The company started to improve its Marketing manuals and brochures by developing a procedure to keep them up-to-date. All of the suggestions were implemented. However, a young woman who spent her spare time investigating online networks like the Internet had an even better idea. She suggested that the company put its manuals, brochures and catalogs online as well. She also suggested creating a CD-ROM for applications and training. This way, updates would be instantaneous, and a customer who was part of the network could receive the latest and best information with a few keystrokes and thus reduce cycle time. The company is even looking at staffing an online service bureau to answer customer questions.

## Summary

### Customer Partnerships

Organizations across the country are moving toward a new relationship with buyers of their products and services. The new breed of customers are known as prosumers because they are actively involved in the production or provision of a product or service which meets their requirements.

### Forecast and Planning

The closer forecasts are to actual demand, the closer you are to achieving maximum cycle time reductions. Planning for production and procurement depends on short-term, accurate forecasting.

### Customer Satisfaction

Customer satisfaction can be quantified and measured in terms of cycle time management. In focusing on areas such as customer delivery performance, a company can reduce cycle time.

### Sales and Field Service

The role of Sales and Field Service is to represent the voice of the customer. The processes in this area must be focused on providing quick and accurate feedback.

### Measurements

Measurements focusing only on dollars spent or dollars earned restrict the process of Cycle Time Management. Measurement systems need to report on nonfinancial activities as well.

# Action Steps

1)  Look at your company's Relationship Map and determine which area of opportunity to tackle first. How can it be improved?

2)  Form a team from Marketing, Sales, Shipping, Customer Service, etc. to determine which elements to map so as to improve customer satisfaction with your company's products and services.

3)  Map each and every element of the task defined as it relates to the overall cycle time.

4)  Begin to measure the variance between starting activities and goals. Brainstorm ways to reduce the deltas.

5)  Develop a customer service assessment study.

6)  Track and measure results in terms of both dollars, time and customer satisfaction.

# Chapter Six:
# Application of
# Principles

In this chapter, we are going to present you with a look at the consulting work we performed for a client who wanted to reengineer customer service centers within its organization. From this discussion, we believe that you will learn the lessons of cycle time management in action. We have identified where cost reductions were achieved and the savings gained from these efforts. You will also see the great amount of teamwork necessary to make an undertaking such as this take off and succeed.

## Process Mapping

Our assignment at this particular company was to develop a team with the objective of generating options for the implementation of integrated work cell designs. We did this by mapping each area of operation in order to analyze the current work flow. These areas included warehouse and distribution centers, mail rooms, clerical units and processing centers. Within each of the areas, our task was to identify potential areas for improvement which included, but was not limited to, queues, batch processing and blockages in the work flow. In addition to mapping the current work flow, we also determined the process time and cycle time for each area. We then developed flow charts depicting the work flows in each area (see Figure 6-1 for a sample "as-is" flow chart) and prepared baseline criteria for the next phase of the process.

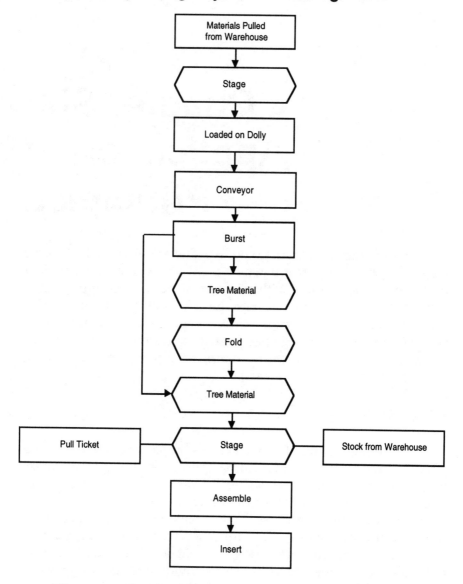

Figure 6-1. Backend Flow

## Assessment and Observations

Our preliminary observations indicated that there were many opportunities for improvement, whether or not the end result for the

114

company was to reengineer into a structure based on cells. In fact, we saw ways in which the company could improve its current operations which could result in readily available cost reductions and efficiency improvements at little or no cost. The team was given the task of studying these opportunities and coming up with plans of action that would take into account any future cell structure implementation.

When we began our consultations, the management team's perspective on the issues was a functional one. This often resulted in a fractured organization which was at odds with itself as objectives in one area conflicted with those in another area. As the team began to explore cell design options, however, we noticed a shift away from focussing on the goals and objectives of each individual function, or department, toward a company-wide view that made satisfaction of the customer the paramount objective.

## Preliminary Issues

The team recognized that the reengineering of their company would create a new environment which would make new demands on the personnel at all levels. With our assistance, they identified several key areas in which company personnel would need to be trained and left themselves open to adding more as the process progressed. The areas that the team thought critical were:

- **Teambuilding.**
- **Working in a team environment.**
- **Total Quality Management.**
- **Sales training.**
- **Inventory management.**
- **Kanban.**
- **Cycle time reduction.**
- **Process mapping.**
- **Benchmarking.**

The team also noted that everybody in the company, no matter what their position, would need to develop the fundamental skills of flexibility and adaptability to be effective in an organization built on a cell structure. In order to determine how strong the work force was in these areas, the team recommended implementing a methodology to assess these skills within the company. The idea behind this recommendation was to begin addressing any weaknesses by starting training programs based on our competency model.

## Primary Recommendations

Our primary recommendation was to eliminate quality assurance as a stand-alone function. At the time, quality assurance was a "checklist and punishment" operation which meant that the objective of QA people was to assure quality, not to improve it. If a worker did what was on his or her list, nothing happened. If they missed something or did it incorrectly, they got a checkmark and were reprimanded. Our suggestion was to find out why procedures were not followed by getting and giving immediate, positive and participatory feedback on quality issues. The purpose was to knock down the walls between quality and the people who do the work. We advised the company to begin making quality improvement a part of each and every operation in a cell center. This would require a paradigm shift in the way both workers and managers thought and acted, but we pointed out that change was necessary since improved quality would increase the satisfaction levels of the customer.

Our second major recommendation was based on our observation of voluminous quantities of paper associated with customer records and orders. At the time, the company had a cumbersome system which required storage in a warehouse. Needless to say, this resulted in considerable delays and multiple handling of customer requests. For example, a customer service request for an historical record check often took three to five days to complete and involved between four and six people. Our advice was to implement a different storage medium, such as microfiche or computerized databases. Such an improved system would save time, research, physical handling and space acquisition. Those cycle time improvements would only serve to improve customer response time and thus increase customer satisfaction levels even more.

## Reengineering the Process

To this point, we have been talking a lot about cell designs and structures. Let's take a look at what they are and how they can help you reduce cycle time as you reengineer your company. The information we are about to provide is the same as what we gave to our client. We thought it would be helpful to itemize a list of characteristics found in an effective and efficient cell structure in order to facilitate the team in the process of cell design. We advised them and are telling you to view these characteristics as baseline benchmarks against which you should measure the suggestions and ideas that come up in team meetings. In other words, if an idea does not promote or advance one or more of these characteristics, then it should probably not be considered for inclusion in the cell structure.

Our list of characteristics includes the following:

- **The structure should be process oriented, not function or product oriented. Your task should be to identify the commonalities between each process in order to simplify the overall process.**

- **Reduce cycle time between each process and within each process. Eliminate the concept of "day" from your thinking. Think, instead, in terms of "hours" or "minutes."**

- **Minimize the distance or connection between each process point. Consider any staging or batching as a constraint to this minimal distance and flow concept.**

- **Work flow should be one-way only. View any rework or reprocessing as counterproductive in an effective and efficient cell design.**

- **Always maximize flexibility in the cell design. Reach for the goal of General Electric — a borderless environment with borderless people. Focus your attention on developing people who are multiskilled and a structural design that is modular in concept or flow.**

- **Seek a process that contains a minimum number of steps with each step being as simple as possible. Use as your guiding principle whether a step adds value to the process.**

- **When designing the cell, consider the personnel skill and the training required. Training must provide consistency and a measurable means for minimizing error.**

# Reengineering Customer Service/Quality Assurance

It's important to do a pilot of any activity. With this in mind, let's take a look now at one specific area which was mapped and studied by a team looking for cycle time reduction opportunities. This area is customer service/quality assurance. Figure 6.2 shows a process map of what occurs when a phone call is received at the company. After observing a customer service center in action and studying the process map, the team identified the following opportunities:

1. **Use personnel to their maximum effectiveness.**
    - **Standardize all phone scripts for less dialogue and digression.**
    - **Strive for better attendance since absences cause standards to fall.**
    - **Continue training program on phone/data entry to minimize delays and uncertainty of operators.**

2. **Streamline work flow.**
    - **Eliminate points at which people pass around the same batch of work.**
    - **Flow paperwork from supervisors to customer service representative areas to final disposition without returning to supervisor/quality assurance areas.**
    - **Install an online error detection system in order to make input and rework quicker and more efficient.**
    - **Use system input to generate tally reports which currently take four hours to prepare correctly.**
    - **Put customer service report online and eliminate need for distributing and filling out paper copies.**
    - **Make inquiry screens available to customer service reps and eliminate need for supervisor to generate, copy and distribute.**

3. **Avoid cluttered areas.**
    - **Downsize the rack and storage areas to allow for better visibility and processing of timely material.**
    - **Allow only authorized people to pull and place materials in staging areas.**

4. **Address supervisory issues.**
   - **Lower operator to supervisor ratio; currently, too many supervisors.**
   - **Start training program on real role of supervisor.**
   - **Adjust supervisor schedule to split shift coverage.**
   - **Download volume-related issues for better scheduling of operators.**

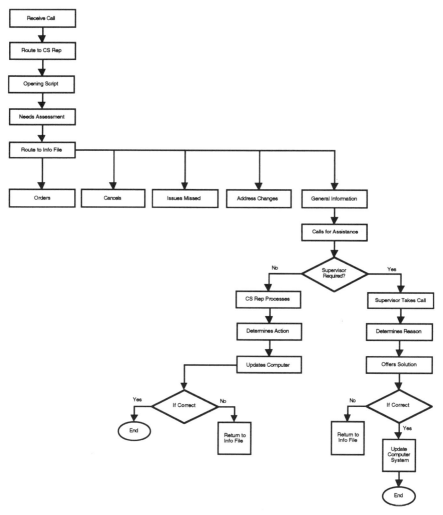

Figure 6-2.

## Reengineering through Cycle Time Management

There was also discussion of implementing prerecorded messages. For example, Press #1 for Address Changes, #2 for Billing Errors, etc. It was believed that this would reduce the number of customer service representatives required, reduce customer delays, improve cycle time and improve customer satisfaction.

We then sat down with the team and showed them how to determine the savings which could be obtained by reducing cycle time for each of these opportunities. In the area of customer service staffing, we found that the return on supervision skills was at best minimal to poor. The company was using four customer service supervisors when only two were justified by the volume of work. By scheduling more effectively, using split shifts and flexible schedules, and implementing peak versus standard workload requirements, we saw that it was possible to reduce the number of supervisors by two for each of the six customer service centers. The savings are shown below:

| Present Situation | Recommended | Reduction | Savings/Year |
|---|---|---|---|
| 4 supervisors (Grade 17) | 2 | 2 | $59,736 (calculated at minimum rate plus 20% for benefits) |

The savings for all six centers would be $358,416 per year.

# Results of Business Reengineering

During the analysis phase of our work at this company, we found that significant savings could be obtained in cycle time, process step and headcount reduction as we helped the organization develop a cell design based on process flow. Our recommendations would achieve the following results:

- Reduce cycle time from 4-14 days to 1-2 days.

- Reduce process steps from 220 total to 105 total.

- Reduce headcount by minimum of 86 people. With capital investments, reduce headcount by additional 60 people in slow season and by 105 more people in the busy season.

The payroll reduction associated with 86 people was $1,444,000. For an additional 60 people, the payroll reduction would be another $1,402,400. As for an additional 105 people during the four-month peak season, the reduction would be $588,000. Total savings from payroll reduction would amount to $3,074, 400 with the expenditure of $1,000,000 in capital investments. This translated into a 30:1 return on investment (ROI). The ROI was still 14:1 even without the capital investments.

# The Implementation Phase

As we moved into the implementation phase, we provided project management support to the team to ensure that the project was completed on time. At a kick-off meeting, the company reviewed and came to a consensus on the final results of the analysis phase, including generic cell designs, macro analysis of the financial implications and redesigned work flows. The team also identified key focus areas critical to the success of the implementation and assigned team leaders to each. The critical areas were:

- **Facilities.**
- **Human Resources.**

- **Organizational Structure.**
- **Communications.**

- **Systems/Technology.**
- **Financial.**

- **Operating Procedures.**
- **Equipment.**

- **Training.**
- **Measurements.**

- **Operations (day-to-day).**
- **New Business.**

- **Definition/Design of Customer Service Center.**

The company's manager then set the first assignment. Within one week, each of the team leaders were to have accomplished the following assignments:

- **Define the key items or critical tasks to complete within the focus area. Prioritize these tasks.**

## Reengineering through Cycle Time Management

- **Identify the subject matter experts or key players within the work force who can be participants on the team.**

Our role was to become, in the words of the company manager, a "true consultant" who assists each team in the definition of tasks and the development of implementation timelines. Everybody agreed that both management and personnel must seize ownership of this project in order to be successful. The teams must believe that improvement is attainable and must feel empowered to bring that improvement about. We told the assembled people that we would no longer provide the same hands-on level of work that we did in the design and analysis phase because that level of assistance would negatively impact on the teams' ability to take control. We pointed out again that our role was now more of a project manager. By doing this, we were able to empower personnel and ready them for upcoming changes. The overall purpose, of course, was to improve the probability of success for the entire project.

# Reengineering Issues

Although the company's management had made great strides in shifting their thinking from a functional focus to a process orientation, there was still more work required in this area. We wanted to be sure that the new cell design of the customer service area was more than a reorganization of functional work areas. To achieve this end, we worked diligently with the various teams to highlight the work flow process. We did this not only to maintain the process orientation, but to ensure that the projected savings would be achieved.

The team also looked at leadership issues, recognizing that some team leaders may not be able to work to the best of their abilities with the new orientation. The team identified several qualities that they thought were critical to the implementation of cell design. One of these qualities was the ability to be a broad thinker and not to be mired in the functional thinking of the past. The team recognized that continuing to think along functional lines would:

- **Jeopardize the implementation timeline.**

- **Jeopardize the savings available through this project.**

- **Potentially increase future costs because of need to rework parts of the process that are too functionally oriented.**

As a further demonstration of what could be achieved if the company addressed these issues, we pointed out that in our initial analysis we discovered a revealing statistic regarding automated processing of the product. Mail that was automatically processed (60% of the total) required only 4% of the workforce to handle it. Automatically processed mail also had a cycle time of no more than 5 hours, whereas manually processed mail had a cycle time of 1.5 to 5 days. A root analysis of the manually processed mail revealed the top two reasons as error-prone forms and too many similar return envelopes. A simple redesign of reader response forms and return evelopes was the solution. We didn't have to point out the great potential for improvement and savings borne out by these statistics.

## Business Reengineering Achievements

The following results are from one customer service center and show achievements in general categories. Each team mentioned above had their own set of achievements and each of these sets were repeated six times for each service center. This gives you an idea of the multiplying effect of cycle time reduction under a business reengineering plan.

| General Area | Improvement |
| --- | --- |
| Turnover | Reduced from 6% overall to 3% overall. **Benefit:** Reduced recruitment and training costs. Higher quality. |
| Work Leveling | Shifted the subscription file update schedules across the week to provide work leveling in the shop. **Benefit:** Reduced equipment and headcount needed to handle volume; eliminated severe peaks. |
| Increased Capacity | Added new equipment with a minimal increase in headcount. Resulted in increases over budgeted capacity of 37% and 23% in the two affected areas. **Benefit:** Increased capacity at minimal cost due to productivity improvements. |

# Reengineering through Cycle Time Management

**Productivity Improvement**

Increased capacity in production areas and decreased expenses.
Benefit: In the first quarter, the customer service center was 5% under expense budget, 5% under budget revenue and over in volumes processed. The figures below are in millions.

|          | Budget   | Actual   | Variance | %   |
|----------|----------|----------|----------|-----|
| Area #1  | 3,634.5  | 4,376.0  | 741.5    | 20  |
| Area #2  | 2,171.8  | 1,821.8  | -350.0   | -16 |
| Area #3  | 3,324.8  | 3,677.7  | 352.9    | 11  |
| Area #4  | 119.8    | 155.1    | 35.3     | 29  |
| Area #5  | 134.1    | 167.4    | 33.3     | 25  |
| Area #6  | 212.7    | 193.6    | -19.1    | -9  |
| Area #7  | 12,327.7 | 14,601.2 | 2,273.5  | 18  |

**Customer Service**

Improved service to customers by decreasing cycle times.
Benefit: Decrease in customer service complaints.

Number of complaints before and after cycle time improvements.

|       | Year 1 | Year 2 | Variance |
|-------|--------|--------|----------|
| Jan.  | 5,020  | 1,612  | -67.9%   |
| Feb.  | 4,655  | 2,004  | -56.9%   |
| Mar.  | 4,772  | 2,104  | -55.9%   |
| Apr.  | 4,501  | 1,856  | -41.2%   |
| May   | 4,838  | 922    | -19.0%   |
| June  | 4,996  | 478    | -9.6%    |
| YTD   | 28,782 | 8,976  | -31.2%   |

Number of claims paid before and after cycle time improvements.

|       | Year 1 | Year 2 | Variance |
|-------|--------|--------|----------|
| Jan.  | 2,814  | 1,744  | -38.0%   |
| Feb.  | 3,312  | 1,807  | -45.4%   |
| Mar.  | 4,152  | 2,660  | -35.9%   |
| YTD   | 10,278 | 6,211  | -39.6%   |

At the time of publishing this book, the Continuous Improvement Process (CIP) was still rolling along, achieving even more savings. As we went to press, the following reengineering activities were in progress:

| General Area | Improvement |
|---|---|
| **Special Job Billing** | **Establish special job billing procedures on the Local Area Network (LAN). Validate that the special jobs are being billed correctly by comparing the billing logs in the service center to the billing reports from Finance. Potential Benefits: Ensure that all special jobs are billed on time. Increased revenue. Increased cash flow.** |
| **New Equipment** | **Four new machines are being tested. Potential Benefits: Currently showing a 53% increase in production compared to previous rates. New equipment is more reliable and less expensive to maintain.** |
| **New Key Entry System** | **A new key entry system is being developed to reduce editing. Potential Benefits: Headcount reduction, more efficient set-up of forms, fewer entry errors.** |

As you can see, the reduction of cycle time is a continuous improvement process. Some of the steps which are necessary to keep this process going have to deal with personnel issues. In the next chapter, we will explore this area in much more detail. Combined with the activities outlined in the previous chapters, attention to human resources will result in still greater achievements.

## Summary

### Reengineering
The process whereby a company reorients itself to a new way of operations with a new organizational design.

### Reengineering through Cycle Time Management

#### Functional Orientation
A view of the organization as a series of departments each of which have a specific function.

#### Process Orientation
A view of the organization in which activities are structured around the flow of work through the company.

#### Cell Design
An effective and efficient organizational structure based on work flow and the reduction of cycle time; a borderless environment with borderless people.

## Action Steps

1) Perform an analysis of your current process with the aim of identifying potential areas for improvement.

2) Identify areas where skills need to be learned to orient your company's people to a process flow perspective.

3) Search for excessive paperwork and devise ways to eliminate the activities or sharply reduce the cycle time currently required.

4) Research cell design and determine how it could be effective in your company.

# Chapter Seven: Combating Resistance

In discussing how Cycle Time Management (CTM) works in relation to various functions within a company, we have shown you a number of ways to identify problems and find solutions. The largest obstacle to the institutionalization of Cycle Time Management will most likely be the corporate culture of your organization. In any organization, people develop a way of doing things and solving problems that seems to work, but that is not always optimal. And such practices are not always conducive to rooting out waste or to reducing and managing cycle times.

Some statistics say that managers and supervisors spend less than 25% of their day doing what they were hired to do. Most of their time is spent putting out fires, expediting, looking for information, and so on. There is also a deep-rooted bias in management which teaches and rewards managers who concentrate solely on fixing problems instead of looking at how to improve processes. Or, as Pete Grieco likes to point out: If you don't make mistakes, you're never going to learn anything. If you're never going to learn by experimenting, you're never going to improve. A company should reward the employee who uncovers problems, since that person is the resident firefighter. The best way to combat resistance is by making team culture and employee empowerment a way of life in your company, a new corporate culture for a new age in business. The tools to combat resistance are essential to the process of reducing cycle time.

That is why we have repeatedly emphasized that Cycle Time Management is not a program, but a process or way of life. The question becomes one of how does your company institutionalize cycle time reduction so that it revamps your present culture. The solution is for a company to find a champion to drive the process to change cultures. Without this person, the road is full of obstacles.

### Reengineering through Cycle Time Management

Pro-Tech can educate and train you; they can facilitate the discussions and the implementation, but you have to own the process. Your company has to put the performance measurements in place which evaluate on the basis of how much they reduce cycle time. Your teams have to incorporate feedback cycles and posting of results to keep the Continuous Improvement Process of the system alive and well. *World Class Measurements* (ISBN 0-945456-05-0; PT Publications, Inc., West Palm Beach, FL) presents a complete view of the measurements which will be required by functions within the company. No one person can do this by himself or herself. The institutionalization of CTM must fit into a company's culture. That can only be done by people who buy in at all levels and across all functions.

## What Needs to Happen — Required Changes

When we talk about an organization changing its culture, what exactly do we mean? What has to change? We have identified two major changes that must be made by companies in order for them to make the transition to a people-powered company:

- **Attitude Change — Management must see people, getting results, as a valuable resource who should be consulted and informed.**

- **Culture Change — The company must adopt proactive rather than reactive management philosophies and create an atmosphere of trust where people are empowered to and involved in reducing cycle times.**

The eventual outcome of this new culture is to develop teams which are self-governing. Such teams don't need to seek management's approval to solve problems. Management's primary job in this new culture is to be an internal "consultant" that helps to facilitate change. The illustration below gives you a clear idea of what we are discussing. Specifically, the graph shows how a team gains responsibility and authority as management releases control.

What follows are some brief definitions of what we mean by each of the elements in Figure 7-1.

- **Authority—ability of a team to budget, to have access to a petty cash fund.**
- **Self-determination—ability of a team to decide what problems to work on and what methods are the best ones to use.**

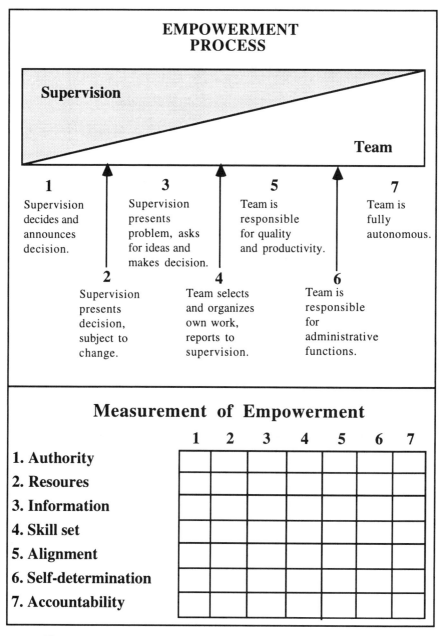

Figure 7-1.

## Reengineering through Cycle Time Management

- **Alignment—a scale which measures how close an employee's personal needs are to the organization's needs.**
- **Skills—the ability of a team to educate and train themselves.**
- **Resources—those items necessary for a team to understand a problem and implement solutions; also, the time to work on solutions, access to manufacturing engineers, etc.**
- **Information—ability of a team to have access to information, computers, financial figures, etc.**
- **Accountability—a scale which measures the level of accountability for a team's actions and results.**

# Resistance to Change

When we have been called in to assess resistance at a company, we have discovered that most problems usually are the result of one of these conditions:

- **Teams believe that TTSP is at work; that is, "this too shall pass," a result of "flavor-of-the-month" management.**

- **Teams believe that management is looking for a scapegoat, somebody or some group to blame for everything that is going wrong.**

- **People believe that the change process is just a way for management to check up on their performance so that people can be laid off.**

- **People know what the problems are and who is causing them, but they can't say because of loyalty to a fellow worker or fear of a supervisor or management.**

- **People have worked in a crisis management environment where change has come to represent out of control conditions. The resultant negative stress leads to behavior in which people avoid the source of change.**

- **Teams are a waste of time. Management never listens to them. Besides, we tried this ten years ago and nothing changed ...**

We advise clients not to suppress these attitudes and feelings, but to bring them out in the open where they can be discussed fully and honestly. Cycle time does reduce work in the organization, as well as create a process for eliminating tasks. Employees are smart and will slow down the cycle time efforts if they don't see the rewards of their labor. Only through honest discussion can you start to build the sense of trust between people and management which is so essential to overcoming any resistance to change as represented by Cycle Time Management. Open discussion of these issues in a team setting is the most effective method of overcoming resistance to change. It is rare to have change successfully imposed from the upper levels of an organization. Resistance to change is most easily met and has the most chance for success as a grassroots process. That means the process of change begins with individual people.

Understanding how people handle change is important. Studies on how people deal with the death of a loved one show that there are five stages that one must go through in order to deal with the death. Psychologists theorize that people go through similar, if not the same, stages when dealing with change in the workplace. The acronym "SARAH" is a memory aid for these five stages.

> S = SHOCK
> A = ANGER
> R = REJECTION
> A = ACKNOWLEDGMENT
> H = HOPE or HELP

Management needs to recognize these phases and encourage people to transition through them in order to become truly empowered.

## Strategy for Change

As we have just said, management should not suppress any of the issues which surround the effects of change. Being competitive in a World Class marketplace means achieving a level of excellence in which strategy shapes and is, in turn, shaped by your corporate culture. Overcoming resistance to change is best met by educating people about the opportunities and benefits from a specific process like cycle time management.

# Reengineering through Cycle Time Management

The first area of attention focuses on developing programs in which managers will learn how to manage change effectively. The second area is the development of orientation programs for all levels of the organization. The goal should be that every person in the company can tell you what CTM is, how it works and what their role is bringing about the change to a new corporate culture. This effort will require the service of a number of cross-functional teams composed of people from the affected disciplines. Many companies have utilized outside consultants like Pro-Tech to speed up the process, in other words, to reduce the cycle time. This is the very thing the whole program is about.

Along with a commitment to education and training, a company must show its commitment by allocating funds to the process of Cycle Time Management. Sounds obvious, but we've seen many companies who don't back up their words with cold, hard cash. When the costs of change are compared with its benefits, it is readily apparent that change is a cost-justified investment. Another necessary ingredient for making the transition is to draw up a list of long-term and short-term objectives to be met as CTM is institutionalized. This list should not be written by management alone, but with the consultation of people at all levels of the company. After these objectives are listed, it is equally important to use your people to determine how the company's efforts will be evaluated and what types of rewards will be given for performance which matches or exceeds stated goals.

Management must realize that results will not always be immediate and that it can take an extended period of time to overcome skepticism. Management must also realize that actions are far more effective than words in convincing people that a long-term commitment is being made. The strategy we advocate rests upon the following principles:

- **Results by example.**
- **Commitment to purpose.**
- **Delivery of commitment through performance.**
- **Dedication to commitment.**

**Results by example.** People learn best when they get feedback about the results of their efforts.

**Commitment to purpose.** This means that all the people in a company understand and accept the goals of the organization. Top management commitment is displayed through their day-to-day behavior. The organizational goals are made visible through ongoing communication among all levels of the organization.

**Delivery of commitment through performance.** With knowledge of the company's goals, management and employees will be able to a continuously improve performance in order to show their commitment to Cycle Time Management.

**Dedication to commitment.** A company mission statement is one way to direct a company's thinking and action toward a common purpose. The test we believe that any company mission statement must pass is this:

**Is the day-to-day behavior of management
and nonmanagement consistent
with the company mission statement?**

# The Basics of Fostering Change

Now that we have looked at some of the behavioral background to resisting change, let's turn to what can be done. We believe that a company needs to pay attention to four basic areas in order to assist in the change process. They are:

- **Motivation training.**
- **Benchmarking training.**
- **Education and training.**
- **Performance measurement training.**

**Motivation.** Motivation operates on two levels — company and personal. At the company level, organizations are motivated to change by competition, cost reduction, new products and the global marketplace. On the personal level, people are motivated by recognition, pay increases, promotions or the fear of being out of a job. Whatever the motivator, it is important to turn it into an area of opportunity. Remember what the philosopher, Plato, said: People change for one of two reasons — fear or hope.

**Benchmarking.** Benchmarking, is the process whereby a company locates pioneer companies in Cycle Time Management and emulates their practices. These companies can provide you with the results to justify change to your employees and guidelines for how to manage the change process itself.

**Education and training**. Although we have repeatedly mentioned education and training as a key to combating resistance, it bears repeating again and again. The skills needed to work together as a team to solve problems and develop opportunities are the most important components of any process of overcoming resistance to change. The aim of education training is to help people internalize behaviors which will be helpful to them and the company.

**Performance measurement**. Performance measurements are critical to the change process when implementing and institutionalizing Cycle Time Management. They act as both a motivator and a feedback mechanism spurring people on to even greater improvements.

With the focus on these four areas, now is the time to formulate a specific strategy for making Cycle Time Management a part of your corporate culture. It will not always be easy, but we have found that companies which stick to the factors outlined below are invariably successful. The list which follows is a blueprint for action to be taken in the first phases of CTM implementation.

### "GETTING STARTED" FACTORS

1) **Establish a vision, i.e., compose a vision statement.**

2) **Assess the company and people in all functions and their readiness for Cycle Time Management.**

3) **Establish a plan to accomplish the creation of a team environment.**

4) **Define short and long range objectives.**

5) **Drive ownership and responsibility to the lowest level.**

6) **Define expectations and set goals.**

7) **Understand the behavioral requirements of people and functions.**

# Some Final Suggestions for Combating Resistance

Leading companies like Motorola, as we have already noted, are always striving to improve, always looking for places where they can get better. Peter Grieco has been an instructor in cycle time management at Motorola University for the past six years. Their commitment to the administration and manufacturing areas is unparalleled. Building on what has been discussed so far, the overall process for implementing a Cycle Time Management process takes the following five basic steps:

1) **Identify areas of opportunity.**
2) **Gather information through organizational surveys.**
3) **Structure the work force into teams.**
    A. **Introduce group dynamic skills.**
    B. **Teach problem-solving skills.**
4) **Facilitate the start-up of teams.**
5) **Institute a performance measurement program and a feedback system.**

Remember that opportunity is not only what management sees as opportunity, but also what the people who work in the organization see as opportunity. When the need for change grows naturally out of the perceptions of people working the soil, then there is a far greater chance that the participative process will take root and flourish.

# Summary

### Corporate Culture
Most likely, the largest obstacle to the institutionalization of Cycle Time Management in any organization. Less than optimal ways of operating a company make it difficult for the sweeping changes of CTM.

### Attitude and Culture Changes
Management should evolve into an internal consultant which empowers employees to develop self-governing teams. Ownership of the process is a key factor in combating resistance to change.

## Reengineering through Cycle Time Management

### Resistance
Don't repress negative attitudes and feelings toward change. Only the full and honest discussion of issues will lessen resistance. Also don't neglect the individual's responses to change. Help people make the transition through the phases of acceptance.

### Long-Term Commitment
Implementation of Cycle Time Management will face skepticism, dissatisfaction with results and growing pains. Management must be committed to seeing the process of change through to ultimate institutionalization.

### Basics of Fostering Change
The four basics of fostering change are: 1) Motivation, 2) Benchmarking, 3) Education and training, and 4) Performance measurement. Upon this foundation, you can build a strategy for change.

# Action Steps

## 10 STEPS FOR OVERCOMING RESISTANCE

1) Obtain information on attitudes and morale.

2) Understand how behavior affects the company and how resistance manifests.

3) Evaluate these attitudes and behaviors.

4) Establish an open-door policy and an open-mind concept.

5) Become an effective listener.

6) Use time effectively to avoid the common pitfall of not enough time to do, listen, collect data, learn.

7) Provide tools — education/training in latest techniques, technologies, etc.

8) Measure results of team activities to demonstrate interest.

9) Reward people/teams for performance stages.

10) Don't procrastinate; make decisions.

# Chapter Eight:
# Administration Cycle
# Time Management

The administrative cycle time of a company is mostly invisible to outsiders and external customers. The tasks which we must accomplish to manage the organization are planned and executed internally. Some of these tasks, which will vary from company and company, are:

- **Strategic business planning.**

- **Accounting and budgeting.**

- **Education and training.**

- **Information technology  management.**

- **Office management and procedures.**

- **Facilities management.**

- **Procurement.**

Administrative cycle time management begins with an analysis of the waste, or nonvalue activity, within your company's organization. You can start by determining how many process steps your company has and by determining whether information flows as it is designated. A well-informed company whose operations have been reengineered to eliminate waste is a well-disciplined company. As

## Reengineering through Cycle Time Management

people truly communicate and work together, administrative coordination develops naturally and wasteful tasks diminish.

The most prevalent forms of administrative waste that we have found at clients are:

- **Unnecessary reports generated at all levels that provide no value to anyone other than the requisitioner.**

- **Unnecessary delays in information and data reporting.**

- **Information systems management.**

- **Errors within the organization.**

- **Equipment downtime — copiers, printers, etc.**

- **Unnecessary approval levels.**

- **Batch processing.**

These areas highlight the major tasks that should be addressed in bringing cycle time under control. It will require reorienting much of our thinking to make the strides required. Instead of lumping administrative costs into an overhead account which everybody accepts as unchangeable, we need to address each cost individually.

# Challenging Administrative Waste

In our consulting work or at our seminars, we often ask companies to explain the relevance of their administrative overhead. We get a number of reactions which range from baffled silence to embarrassment to gung-ho explanations of why administrative overhead is irrelevant. We fall somewhere in the middle. Administrative overhead does serve a purpose in the standard cost equation. But we also notice that a great number of the components of overhead are actually additional process step activities disguising themselves as overhead so that they won't attract your attention. If it is your company's desire to become World Class, then you must focus on cycle time reduction. Companies that identify these critical components are finding opportunities for cost reduction.

We have been talking a lot about waste, but what exactly is it? This is the definition that we use:

---

**WASTE**

**Anything other than the minimum resources
of people, machines, or materials
that add value to products.**

---

Is the cost of this administrative waste relevant? (And by cost, we mean both in terms of dollars and time.) The answer is yes. Waste affects product cost which affects margins which affects profits which determine the success of your company. Take a moment right now and consider the activities performed in your organization that are part of the administrative cycle. Start by thinking about a specific function such as sales, engineering, quality, finance, maintenance, materials management, or shipping. Are the activities within a specific function adding value to the product or service your company builds or provides? If they aren't, then they need to be evaluated and either reduced or eliminated. As always, we recommend forming a team of people who will take their clipboards and visit the targeted function. There, the team will gather data and investigate administrative cycle time activities.

As an example of what we mean, let's imagine that you have selected the Purchasing function of your company as the area in which you will challenge administrative cycle time. First you would determine the day-to-day administrative activities that take place in Purchasing, such as the typical ones depicted below.

- **Phone Calls — Internal and External**
- **Requisition Processing**
- **Retrieving MRP Order Action Reports**
- **Entering Purchase Orders**
- **Distributing and Filing Paper**
- **Mailing Orders**
- **Expediting Activities**
- **Data Base Maintenance**

# Reengineering through Cycle Time Management

- **Meetings — Internal Planning**
- **Meetings with Suppliers**
- **Performing Surveys and Audits**
- **Purchase Order Changes**
- **Supplier Reschedules**
- **Matching Invoices**
- **No PO Status Recievers**

After the list of activities is completed, the team then can utilize Process Mapping Software to develop the Process and Relationship maps which we discussed earlier in the book. These maps will help them identify bottlenecks and disconnects which plague the activities above. The overall cycle time reduction strategy is to use cross-functional, self-directed and empowered teams to root out waste. The best method of gaining productivity improvements in administration is to use the same people involvement that you would use on the factory floor. The principles are the same. The people on "the front lines" are the ones best able to find the areas which can be improved. By using the two guidelines below, teams can uncover a great many opportunities for cost reduction:

1) **Evaluate all paperwork. Ask the question "Why?" five times. Can we eliminate, reduce or consolidate forms, memos, letters, etc.?**

2) **Observe lines of authority. Can we delegate more responsibility to lower levels of the organization?**

One attitude problem that you may need to overcome in administrative cycle time is the belief that productivity improvement is not that important to the bottom line of the company. Bureau of Labor Statistics, however, show that productivity in administration in recent years has either declined or moved forward at an infinitesimal rate. Meanwhile, competition in the global marketplace has leaped ahead in this area. That should be reason enough to start bringing administrative cycle time under control.

Control, of course, begins with measurement. Consider, for example, how much money your company could save if you could reduce the number of journal voucher errors. But in order to start reducing this waste, you must begin with a baseline. We recommend that changes made to vouchers be tablulated in some manner or by the computer system which already logs them. The responsibility for this measurement should be with the individuals performing the voucher entry function. With a baseline established, you can then use teams to look at the steps and then begin to brainstorm alternative methods which could consolidate, reduce or eliminate activities.

# Information Management

Much of the improvement you eventually make in controlling administrative cycle time will depend on the way your company manages information. Information system management is vital to your company's ability to attain World Class status. Many companies, unfortunately, have difficulty accurately describing what types of hardware and software applications they use and who are the personnel who use the tools provided by the system. It is important to select a business solution for systems that supports your objectives over the next five years.

The foundation of Cycle Time Management is the ability to capture and process quantities of day-to-day data and paperwork, such as invoices, purchase orders, stock movements, shipping documents, etc. These systems must record the data, provide timely information on customer status — on-hand, on order, delivery — and, perhaps more importantly, update systems which are then used as input to higher levels of planning and control. We are trying to get to activity-based costing systems.

Well-designed information systems are instrumental in reporting data on time and gaining control of administrative cycle time. A sound system design starts with a team making an accurate assessment of your company's requirements. It then will need to evaluate your present system and find ways to improve it or replace it. A way to begin looking at your present information system technology is to review the following topics:

**HARDWARE**

1. **CPU:**

   Manufactured by_____Model_____

   Memory Size:_____

141

# Reengineering through Cycle Time Management

2. Disk Capacity _____

3. Tape Drives:  (Model/Quantity) _____

4. Printers:  (Model/Quantity) _____

5. Terminals:  (Model/Quantity) _____

6. Local Area Network _____

7. Personal Computers _____

8. Documentation _____

9. Policy and Procedures _____


## SOFTWARE

1. Operating System _____

2. Database Management System _____

3. Communications Software _____

4. Local Area Network _____

5. Financial _____

6. MRP/MRP II _____

7. Forecasting _____

8. CAD/CAM _____

9. Repetitive _____

10. Distribution _____

11. Graphics _____

12. Word Processing _____

13. Electronic Mail _____

14. EDI _____

15. Revision Number _____

16. Documentation _____

17. Other _____

## PERSONNEL

1. Programmers (Number/Experience) _____

2. Systems Analysts (Number/Experience) _____

3. Computer Operators (Number/Experience) _____

4. How many "users" operate the computer _____

## APPLICATIONS

1. Number of Data Transactions Daily _____

2. EDI Applications _____

3. Real-time or Batch Process _____

4. System Response Time _____

# Putting It All Together

How does all that we have said so far fit together? Let us give you an example based on Peter Grieco's experience while working as director of operations at the Apple Macintosh plant in Freemont, California. Cycle Time Management had been part of Pete's philosophy for a long time. The following is a summary of the methods he used to bring administrative cycle time under control.

First of all, I recognized that we needed a vision of what we could accomplish. If that wasn't clear to me, then there was no way for me to get the excitement across to the people who worked with me. I had to communicate my vision in order to gain the support or buy-in that would be necessary to attack administrative cycle time. All the talk in the world, of course, is useless if you are not going to let people own their part of the whole. I had seen too many managers and supervisors who let their egos get in the way of doing the job right. A manager is not judged on how many good ideas he or she has or even on how well the ideas are communicated. We are judged on results, and that means we need the cooperation and the enthusiasm of people who work with us.

Success, then, is based on how well a manager allows the people in a department to assume responsibility and exercise authority. In a way, the success of a World Class manager is how well he or she relinquishes control to others.

While at Apple, we were constantly engaged in the management of administrative cycle time. I tried to become an effective leader by recognizing the importance of people as innovators and as individuals. I saw one of my primary functions as being a team developer. This meant that I needed to let people know that I trusted them and that they could fail, if they could learn from their mistakes. Somebody once said that almost every important invention was accomplished by the wrong person at the wrong time and for the wrong reason. When people have the courage to go against the grain and ask "Why?" every time they hear the same old explanation, that's when we will have progress.

Anybody who has met me knows that "Why?" is my favorite word. Some people think I ask that question just to be a pain and that I don't care what they have to say. Nothing could be further from the truth. I'm waiting for somebody to give me an answer, an answer that leaves me satisfied. When I see somebody hemming and hawing, I know that they haven't thought out the problem. If they had, they could tell me why I should accept what they say.

I believe that the use of teams is the best way to come up with answers to the question "Why?" That's because a good team is composed of members trained in problem-solving techniques. In essence, they have already learned how to ask "Why?" several times. I strongly believe that people will do their work more efficiently and intelligently if management lets them use their brains to their fullest capacities. That's the best way to reduce administrative cycle time.

# Summary

### Administrative Cycle
Tasks planned and executed internally to manage an organization. The administrative cycle of a company is mostly invisible to outsiders and customers. Administrative cycle time management begins with an analysis of the waste in your company's organization.

### General Areas of Opportunity
It is important to recognize that we can reduce the cycle time it takes to perform a task in all areas of business. Opening the mail, receiving or sending faxes, planning meetings, emptying the trash in the office can all save your company money by reducing the cycle time.

Each of you can probably make a list of numerous things to do. The issue at hand will be what you can do based on your work load and time availabity. We can only advise you that you have to start someplace, so start now.

# Action Steps

1) Educate and train your employees in the use of fishbone diagrams as part of an overall problem-solving program which is taught to all levels of your organization.

2) Use the Information Management assessment in this chapter to rate the effectiveness of your hardware and software. Also draw Process Maps of the administrative flow of information. Study these maps and look for bottlenecks and disconnects.

3) Form a steering committee with the mission of challenging administrative waste through teams which will address individual opportunities for improvement.

4) Get education and training in Activity Based Costing to assist you in assigning costs to administrative tasks with the ultimate goal of reducing or eliminating them altogether.

# Chapter Nine:
# Finance Cycle Time
# Management

We have found that the majority of waste in finance cycle time is evidenced by policies and procedures, inaccurate data and measurements and the normal month-end crisis. The purpose behind finance cycle time reduction is to use finance resources to create a more proactive business partnership role. This can be achieved by significantly reducing time wasted on handling and processing data, by making processes seamless and invisible and by implementing high quality systems which generate just-in-time information, not just-in-case data.

Motorola took these steps and was able to reduce the cycle time for closing books at the end of the month from *21 days* to just *one day*. The company began by reducing the cycle time of core financial cycles: month-end closing, customer invoicing, forecasting and customer reporting. They also focused on eliminating nonvalue-added reporting. It should be recognized that the Information Service area could not change and process data to keep up with the financial team.

One of the areas addressed and tackled by Motorola during this process was the generation of reports and charts. There were three questions that the company asked itself to determine whether some of these items were necessary to the month-end closing. They were as follows:

- **Does the report or chart add value to the product or service provided to the customer?**
- **Does the report or chart add value to the process of satisfying the customer?**
- **Does the report or chart support the company's key initiatives?**

They experienced an estimated 75% reduction in paper consumption as a result of their efforts in the cycle time effort.

# Challenging Finance Waste

The following flow charts demonstrate some powerful ways of reducing cycle time in your financial areas. Use these diagrams as a means to stimulate your own ideas for reducing cycle time in your organization.

The backbone of the general A/P process, as depicted in Figure 9-1, is to receive a PO and mail a check with a minimum number of steps. The only necessary steps are to perform an audit which matches the PO with the invoice and then generate a check which can be signed before being sent out. Much of this process can be computerized.

As for reengineering the finance cycle of cash application and A/R management, we also seek to reduce cycle time. In Figure 9-2, you can see that this process begins with either updating or monitoring compliance with credit policy. Upon investigation and approval, a new customer can be set up and the process of collections can begin after credits, debits and deductions are issued and resolved. The process of managing and reporting cash and A/R aging continues up to the point where transfers and journal vouchers are made and entered.

Figure 9-3 shows in detail the process whereby a credit application is investigated and approved. The first checkpoint determines whether the application is complete. If it is, a financial test is applied in which more credit information is obtained. Eventually, approvals are sought and the process ends.

Figure 9-4 also depicts the process of new customer set-up/ change in more detail. The steps in this process are first to determine if the form is complete. When it is, the information is then entered into the system and sales/order entry are alerted of the changes or new set-up.

The cash application process in Figure 9-5 depicts how checks are sorted and input into the system. The list is then edited and if it is correct, the cash is posted and information recorded in the cash log book.

Figure 9-6 shows the steps involved in preparing a cash report. Basically, information from sales, credit, payroll, A/R and A/P are

channeled into one area. The chart in this figure shows the interme-
diate steps and how they interconnect.

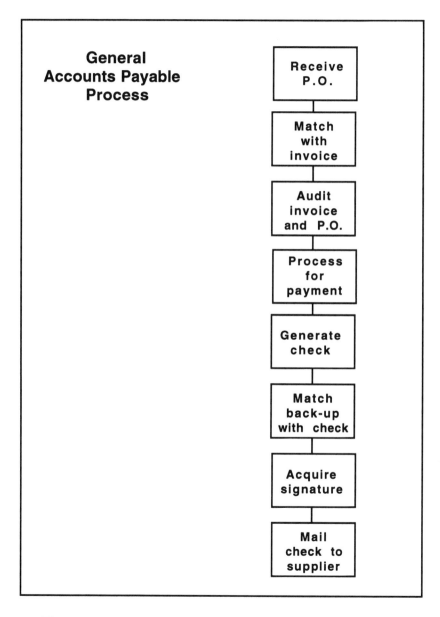

Figure 9-1.

# Reengineering through Cycle Time Management

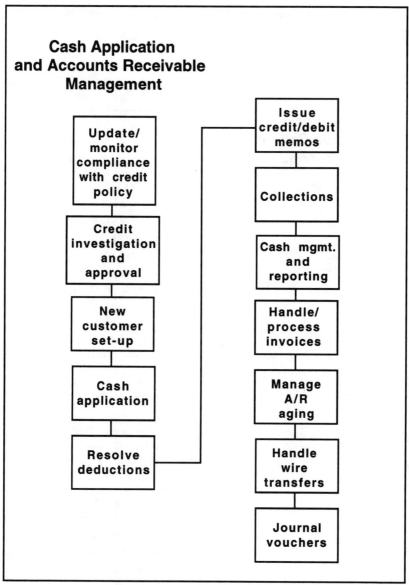

Figure 9-2.

150

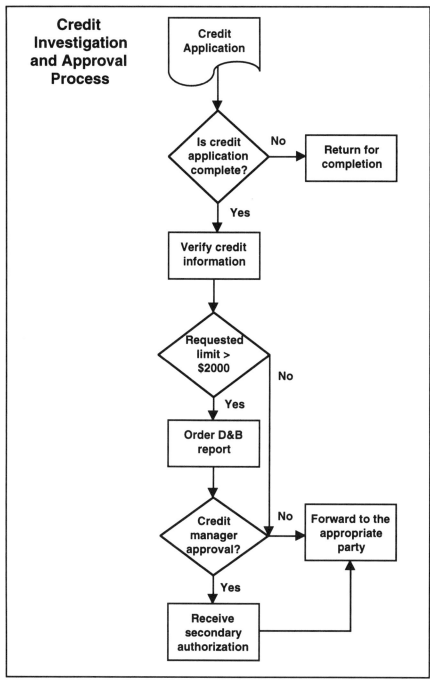

**Credit Investigation and Approval Process**

Credit Application

Is credit application complete? → **No** → Return for completion

↓ **Yes**

Verify credit information

Requested limit > $2000 → **No** →

↓ **Yes**

Order D&B report

Credit manager approval? → **No** → Forward to the appropriate party

↓ **Yes**

Receive secondary authorization

Figure 9-3.

151

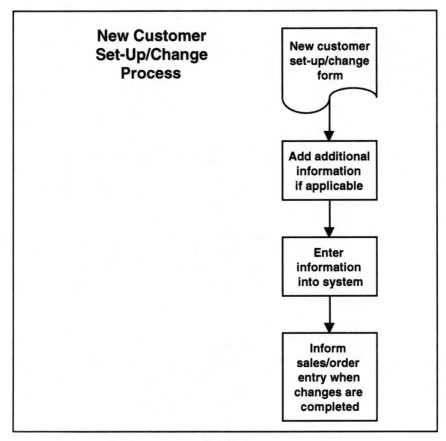

Figure 9-4.

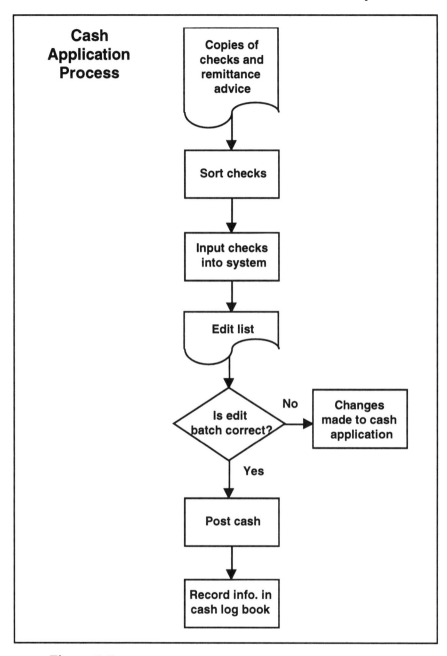

Figure 9-5.

# Reengineering through Cycle Time Management

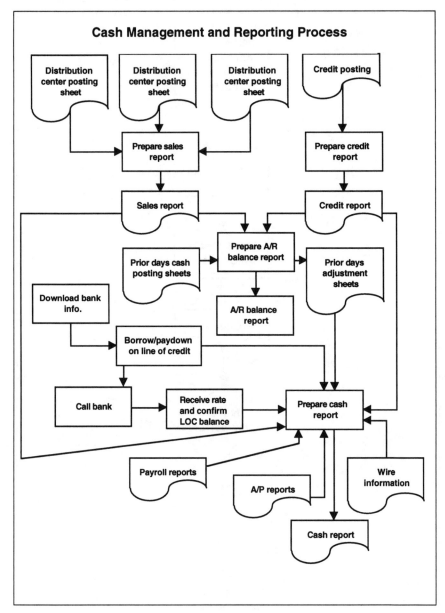

**Figure 9-6.**

What these flow charts demonstrate so well is the accomplishments that can be achieved when an effort is made to reduce the number of steps in a process or to eliminate steps entirely when the

154

opportunity arises. The achievement of World Class status will require a company to streamline the General Ledger process. New software systems such as Oracle™ have designed General Ledger systems which generate financial statement reports that allow executives to truly use data to make decisions.

Traditional General Ledger models are primarily formatted and developed to produce financial results for external purposes. However, the type of results that we are looking for internally are captured as aggregate totals and buried in the General Ledger. Companies are recognizing the value of segregating this data in order to run the organization more efficiently and cost effectively. New finance systems should provide companies with cost categories that distinguish between value-added and nonvalue-added costs. This break down will support opportunities to involve everyone in cycle time reduction. The assessment that we use will stimulate your thought process to view the finance function differently and start that reengineering process of cycle time reduction.

1. **How many account numbers in Chart Of Accounts?**_____
   **What is the format?**_____
   **Is there significance?**_____
   **Are there interfaces to other accounting systems?**_____
2. **When does the financial year end?**_____
   **How many periods are there?**_____
3. **How long does it take to produce period end reports?**_____
   **How long does it take to produce year end reports?**_____
   **What additional processes are required at year end?**_____
4. **Is there a formal budgeting process?**_____
   **Cash budget?**_____ **Capital budget?**_____
5. **Is the budget used to control expenses at the department level?**_____
6. **How many people are primarily involved with:**

| ACCOUNTING FUNCTION | NO. OF PEOPLE |
| --- | --- |
| General Accounting | _____ |
| Cost Accounting | _____ |
| Accounts Payable | _____ |
| Accounts Receivable | _____ |
| Controller | _____ |
| Payroll | _____ |
| Treasurer | _____ |
| Other | _____ |

# Reengineering through Cycle Time Management

7. How are indirect costs allocated?_____

8. What financial reports are currently being prepared?
   _____

9. Define the opportunities in the Financial area for improvement:
   _____
   _____
   _____

10. Does all data flow to the General Ledger?
    _____Yes    _____No

11. How is justification of cost taking place today?
    _____
    _____
    _____

12. How are performance measurements extracted from the General Ledger?
    _____
    _____
    _____

13. Does the system include an allocation process to develop cost elements using any of the following?
    **Splits:**
    By product _____
    By work cell_____
    By department _____
    **Spreads:**
    Percent_____
    Weighted average_____
    Other calculation_____
    **Statistics:**
    Head count _____
    Square footage_____
    Transactions_____
    Other (name)_____

14. Is data from the General Ledger used for performance measurements?
    _____Yes    _____No
    If yes, list:
    _____
    _____
    _____

### JIT DELIVERY TO JIT PAYMENT

Finance cycle time reduction will mean connecting JIT delivery to JIT payment. New bank systems utilizing credit cards for small purchases have greatly reduced the paperwork in both purchasing and finance. Almost all the major financial institutions offer these cards to companies with excellent track records. This will not only improve supplier relations, but eliminate much paperwork for Finance. This double-sided benefit is not possible until a company can convince Finance to eliminate invoices for every shipment, especially if they are daily. Finance may look at a JIT payment schedule and see not less paperwork, but decidedly more. The practices of including a check as part of the PO for small purchases, using Purchase Credit Cards, backflushing and payment at time/point of use of supplier material are examples of World Class practices that further simplify processes. In a company which has achieved World Class status, it is possible to eliminate matching invoices because it has guaranteed daily shipment of quality parts through a Supplier Certification program. EDI and bar coding applications can greatly help Finance in this regard. A Japanese company successfully receives 2,000 different components a day with the use of bar coding technology in Receiving and Accounts Payable.

Companies must look at Accounts Payable from a total cost approach, hooking purchasing and finance together at the hip. If a company loses a month of interest because it paid more quickly, then consider how much more money it will have saved by quickly shipping to its customer and by lowering its inventory cost. The issue is to pay on time, collect on time and use cash effectively. This will be a major change for most companies. Here are some additional questions for you to consider:

1. **Are the same A/P methods used for nonproduction material (i.e., supplies) as for production materials?** _____

    Explain: _____

    _____

2. **Are invoices matched against receipts and purchase orders?**

    _____

3. **Are cash requirements forecasted for future periods?** _____

# Reengineering through Cycle Time Management

4. Is there a method used to take advantage of supplier discounts?
   Explain: _____

   _____
5. How often are A/P invoices paid?_____
6. How are special checks handled?
   COD _____
   Manual _____
   Prepayment _____
7. Is there a detailed check voucher for each check?_____
8. Are checks prenumbered?_____
9. How is reconciliation of paid checks handled?_____

   _____
10. How are returns to suppliers handled?_____
11. Is there an adequate method of security on confidential supplier information?

    _____

    Explain: _____

    _____
12. Flow today's A/P process from receipt through check payment.

    _____

    _____
13. How are the following application used or planned in A/P?
    Bar Coding? _____

    _____

    _____

    Kanban?_____

    _____

    _____

    EDI?_____

    _____

    _____
14. How are the costs of administering A/P collected?
    Overhead?_____
    Allocation to product?_____
15. What is the average age of the A/P function?
    ____ 0-30 ____ 31-60 ____ 61-90 ____ 91>
16. Define areas of opportunity.

    _____

    _____

    _____

## ACCOUNTS RECEIVABLE

As in the area of Accounts Payable, we must work with our customers to pay on a timely basis. Application of EDI, bar coding and various new methods will require our financial people to work with customers in the future. World Class involvement means cleaning up the paper process as the following questions demonstrate.

1. How many customers are on file?_____
   Number active in last 12 months?_____
   Are customer numbers assigned?_____
2. Is customer history maintained by product?_____
   Service parts?_____ Total sales dollars?_____
   Other_____
3. How is credit worthiness determined, maintained, and communicated?
   _____
   _____
4. Is there an adequate method of security on confidential customer information?_____
   _____
5. How often are invoices prepared?_____
   Are they prenumbered?_____
6. How are special invoices handled?_____
7. How are customer returns handled?_____
8. How often is cash applied?_____
9. How often are receivables aged?_____
   Is a trial balance prepared?_____
10. What are average outstanding A/R balances?

| | | | |
|---|---|---|---|
| Current | _____ | Over 90 | _____ |
| Over 30 | _____ | Over 120 | _____ |
| Over 60 | _____ | | |

11. Where are standard discount terms?_____

# Chapter Ten:
# Computers in Cycle
# Time Management

It's a given that the business world is changing and that we can all expect hard-nosed global competition, higher customer expectations and rapid technological changes. All of which means that companies will need to transform themselves from slow-moving hierarchies into lean, service-driven firms that focus on total customer satisfaction and cycle time reduction. And the way for companies to undergo this process is to take up the cause of reducing cycle time through reengineering efforts.

There are software packages, such as Process Vision, which provide industrial strength tools for companies engaged in business process reengineering (BPR). They enable users to visually analyze, document and transform business processes, policies and procedures by providing streamlined software that allows you to create accurate pictures of current activities (as-is) and roadmaps for improved organizational processes (should-be). With a visually-based format, these software packages have helped consultants, quality groups and analysts to achieve millions of dollars in savings, faster time-to-market and higher levels of customer satisfaction in industries as diverse as finance, insurance, manufacturing, retail, telecommunications and more.

## Fulfilling Business Needs

By providing an accurate, complete picture of a company's existing procedures and policies, these powerful software products

## Reengineering through Cycle Time Management

can help organizations reduce cycle time, flatten hierarchies, improve customer service, and become lean and agile. In the past, this was a time-consuming task, involving paper-and-pencil interviews, string-and-pin diagrams and hit-or-miss assumptions. The result was a final analysis of the company which was flawed by missing elements and inconsistent information.

Software can eliminate these flaws by capturing and analyzing an accurate cross-functional view of your organization. It can document and validate all the factors in each of your company's business activities, answering the questions of "who," "what," "where," "when," and "how." Then the software gives you a graphical representation of all of the factors which impact competitiveness. But that's not all. The software should also support various types of detailed reports, including workflow, cycle time, dataflow and policy analyses.

# How BPR Software Works

BPR software is based on the concept of undertaking a project at the field or form level. Different tasks allow users to document and map each activity of the organization and produce reports and graphical displays which show elapsed time in the workflow and links to the other functions in the organization. The software also allows you to build models to test different configurations in "what if" cases.

The software allows you to facilitate the complete and unbiased collection of information concerning processes and procedures. You will be prompted, for example, to collect relevant data concerning job functions and workflows, as well as policies, information flow, internal structure and interfaces with other processes and organizations.

A key feature is the ability to show this data in a visual format as you collect it. This allows you to work with interviewees and to respond to their input immediately. You are then able to fine-tune views of the business and eliminate any later misunderstandings or misinterpretations. The software allows you to automatically validate and error check to uncover inconsistencies and missing information. Since the primary purpose of BPR software is to focus on the workflow and produce graphical representations of current "as-is" and reengineered "to-be" processes, these automated features should make sure that no processes are left unaccounted for. The result will be complete closure in all activities.

Current processes should then be able to be viewed simultaneously with reengineered processes, providing an intuitive roadmap for maximizing the productivity and competitiveness of your company. The software also allows you to analyze the "what-if" advantages and drawbacks of various procedural changes.

Yet another necessary feature of BPR software is that it should give you the ability to "drill-down" through each process to get additional detailed information on procedures, accountability and resources. This graphical view can help you pinpoint exact weaknesses in each process and develop an action plan for continuous improvement.

Other features include the ability to generate:

- **Job procedure manuals.**

- **Business process event response models.**

- **Activity frequency, volume and timing information.**

- **Resource utilization levels.**

- **Policy-to-process mapping information.**

# Process Vision in Action

Let's look at one of these software packages in more detail in order to see how it benefits those who are in the process of reducing cycle time. Process Vision has been used by the retail, chemical, energy, insurance, manufacturing, government, banking, utilities and communications industries. Some of the companies which have used the software include AT&T, Mitsubishi, Bethlehem Steel, Enron, Dow Chemical and the Department of Defense. To give you an idea of what can be accomplished with Process Vision, consider the story of one steel producer as reported by the software developer.

"At this particular company, the transportation department was considering going to an Executive Shipment Settlement System (ESS) method of paying freight bills. This type of system is

# Reengineering through Cycle Time Management

designed to send a check to the freight carrier once the truck or rail car leaves the shipping dock. This contrasted with the currently used method of paying freight bills whereby a check was sent to the carrier after an invoice had been received.

"The goals of the team studying this problem with Process Vision were to:

- **Develop a thorough understanding of and documentation of the freight payment process.**
- **Identify inefficient job functions and recommend improvements.**
- **Determine the feasibility of an ESS system.**

"The six team members took two months to review the project and came up with two levels of recommendations. The first level included sixteen recommendations that were relatively low in cost and short in time frame to implement. The second level included implementing all of the first level and increasing the use of an already existing electronic data interchange (EDI) system. The final action was that an ESS system was not recommended because it would have been too costly to implement. Implementation of level one recommendations would decrease freight payment effort per year by 20% and the increased use of EDI along with level one recommendations would decrease the effort by 76%."

Yet another example of the power of Process Vision from their company literature can be seen in this example. "A customer assistance center of a communications company was frequently missing the established target time for completing a Trouble Ticket. A Trouble Ticket was created when a customer called and reported a problem with their service. A technician answered the call and responded by isolating and analyzing the problem and taking the appropriate steps to repair the trouble.

"The goals of the team studying this problem were to:

- **Evaluate the processes supporting the generation of a Trouble Ticket, that is, the handling of Trouble Calls.**

- **Determine the reasons the Customer Assistance Center was missing the established cycle time targets (response time was supposed to be within 24 hours).**

164

- **Recommend solutions so that the Center could meet the established target times.**

"Within four months, the six team members came up with fifty recommendations by using the Process Vision software. Each recommendation provided the amount of time that would be saved. One of the recommendations identified a lack of adequate staffing at peak customer calling periods and overstaffing during slower periods. In addition, the technicians available at peak times did not have the experience or background necessary to deal with complicated customer needs. Identifying and rectifying these problems resulted in the average response time dropping from 23 hours to ½ hour.

"Process Vision also provided job narratives which aided in documenting methods and procedures for current job tasks. Having the job tasks in an electronic format allowed them to be updated quickly which eliminated several weeks of development time from the present documentation procedure."

There are many other examples of the power of Process Vision. As you can see, BPR software is a very powerful tool in the Continuous Improvement Process.

# Additional Purchasing Resources
# from PT Publications, Inc.

**3109 45th Street, Suite 100**
**West Palm Beach, FL 33407-1915**

<u>PROFESSIONAL TEXTBOOKS</u>

*MADE IN AMERICA: The Total Business Concept*
Peter L. Grieco, Jr. and Michael W. Gozzo

Full of case studies, charts, tables, tactics and strategies. *302 pages*

*JUST-IN-TIME PURCHASING: In Pursuit of Excellence*
Peter L. Grieco, Jr., Michael W. Gozzo and Jerry W. Claunch

"...must reading for purchasers and every level of management that are just starting or intending to pursue JIT." — *Electronic Buyers News*. *199 pages*

*SUPPLIER CERTIFICATION II: A Handbook for Achieving Excellence through Continuous Improvement*
Peter L. Grieco, Jr.

Over 20,000 copies sold worldwide. Most effective when used with our *Supply Management Toolbox*. *549 pages*

*BEHIND BARS: Bar Coding Principles and Applications*
Peter L. Grieco, Jr., Michael W. Gozzo and C.J. (Chip) Long

Find out how bar coding can work for you. *244 pages*

## Reengineering through Cycle Time Management

*SET-UP REDUCTION: Saving Dollars with Common Sense*
Jerry W. Claunch and Philip D. Stang

Step-by-step guide to implementing and institutionalizing set-up reduction in your company. Save money now! *309 pages*

*WORLD CLASS: Measuring Its Achievement*
Peter L. Grieco, Jr.

"The best holistic measurement book around." — Carl Cooper, Senior Applications Consultant for Motorola University. *287 pages*

*THE WORLD OF NEGOTIATIONS: Never Being a Loser*
Peter L. Grieco, Jr. and Paul G. Hine

How to master the art of world class negotiations. *242 pages*

*PEOPLE EMPOWERMENT: Achieving Success from Involvement*
Michael W. Gozzo and Wayne L. Douchkoff

Learn how and why to empower your employees so as to net the most success from their involvement. *288 pages*

*ACTIVITY BASED COSTING: The Key to World Class Performance*
Peter L. Grieco, Jr. and Mel Pilachowski

Develop and implement a costing system which provides information to make your company more efficient and profitable. *243 pages*

*SUPPLY MANAGEMENT TOOLBOX: How to Manage Your Suppliers*
Peter L. Grieco, Jr.

The companion book to *Supplier Certification II*. All the forms and charts you need to get your process up and running. *344 pages*

*POWER PURCHASING: Supply Management in the 21st Century*
Peter L. Grieco, Jr. and Carl R. Cooper

A practical guide for companies who want to understand the paradigm shift in Purchasing. *204 pages*

*GLOSSARY OF KEY PURCHASING TERMS, ACRONYMS, AND FORMULAS*
PT Publications

The latest terms in the field of purchasing are explained and detailed.

## VIDEO EDUCATION SERIES

*SUPPLIER CERTIFICATION: The Path to Excellence*

A nine-tape series on World Class Supplier Based Management. The best explanation in its field.

## AUDIO PROFESSIONAL EDUCATION TAPES

*THE WORLD OF NEGOTIATIONS: How to Win Every Time*

A leading edge audio tape on developing a negotiating strategy based on Total Cost, Total Quality Control, Just-In-Time and world class relationships. Focus is on a company-wide strategy. Nobody else has a tape like this.

To find out more about our extensive offerings,
give us a call at 1-800-272-4335.

# Index

**A**
ABB 82
Accounts payable process 149
Accounts receivable management 150, 159
Activity based costing 22-23
Administrative cycle time 137-138
Administrative waste 138-141
Agile manufacturing 11-13
Apple Computer 103, 143
Attitude change 128

**B**
Becker, Joe 58
Benchmarking 25, 47-50
Bennetton 11-12
BPR software 162-163
Business process reengineering 161

**C**
CAD/CAM 44
Cash application process 153
Cash management and reporting process 154
Cellular operations 55, 58-63
Concurrent engineering 38-44
Continuous improvement process 6-8
Cost/benefit analysis 77
Credit investigation process 151
Culture change 128
Customer complaints 110
Customer satisfaction 104-105
Customer service/quality assurance 118-120
Customer set-up/change process 152

Cycle time achievements  10
Cycle time management, definition of  3-6
Cycle time reduction  9-11
Cyrix Corporation  106-108

**D**
Design and development cycle time  33
Design and development stages — traditional  34-35
Design and development stages — simultaneous
    methodology  35-38
Designing for producibility  44-46

**E**
Early customer involvement  95-98
Early supplier involvement  46-47, 89
Empowerment process  15, 129
External cycle time  90-91

**F**
Factory America Net  76
Federal Express  108
Feigenbaum, Armand V.  63
Finance waste  148-149, 154-156
First steps  23-28
Forecast and planning  101-103

**G**
Goldhar, Joel  97
Gore, Al  76
Grieco, Peter L., Jr.  22, 58, 66, 103, 127, 135, 143-145
Group technology  55, 58-63

**H**
Hat Brands  58
Heileman Brewing  63-64

**I**
Implementation  121-122
Information management  141-143
Information technologies  75-77

Institutionalizing 13-18
Inventory management 71-74

**J**
J.I. Case 67
JIT payment 157-158
Just-in-time 74

**K**
Kanban 65-67

**L**
Levi Strauss 14, 16
L.L. Bean 5, 108

**M**
Management techniques 17
Manufacturing technologies 54-55
Marketing/sales/customer service cycle time 94-95
Measurements 108-110
Mission statement 8-9
Motorola 4, 8, 97, 108, 147
MTBF 31

**N**
National Bicycle Industrial Company 33
Neodata 68-70

**O**
Opportunities, cycle time 20-22
Oracle 155
Order entry 98-101

**P**
Paradigm shift in manufacturing 55-57
Paulk, Ken 58
Pilachowski, Mel 22, 60
Power purchasing 81-89
Process map 25, 27, 113-114
Process Vision 82, 161, 163-165

Product development cycle  10
Pro-Tech  13
Purchasing flow  82-89

**R**
Reengineering  116-117, 120-121, 122-125
Relationship map  24-26
Resistance to change  130-131, 136
Robotics and automation  74-75

**S**
Sales and marketing  106-108
Saturn (General Motors)  11-12
Set-up reduction  67-70
Six sigma  9
Statistical process control  63, 65
Stec, Bob  58
Strategy  23-24
Strategy for change  131-135
Supplier partnerships  89-90

**T**
Theoretical cycle time  4
Total productive maintenance  70-71
Total quality control  74

**W**
Wal-Mart  11-12
White spaces  17-18
World Class assessments  18-19
World Class measurements  19-22

**X**
Xerox  5